DAD'S
SIMPLE
FUN
MAGIC

GUIDE TO WALT DISNEY WORLD PLANNING

CARL (DAD) TRENT

Dad's Simple Fun Magic Guide to Walt Disney World Planning
© 2017 by Carl Trent. All rights reserved.

Publisher: CTSA LLC
Designer: Stephanie Shuster
Pigment Illustrations: Jamie Cosley

ISBN: 978-0-9992550-0-1

First Edition
Published in the United States of America

REGISTER YOUR BOOK

READ THIS FIRST!

Dad's Simple, Fun, Magic Guide to Walt Disney World Planning
is more than just a book - it's a complete vacation planning tool!
By registering your book, you'll gain access to a special members-only
website with helpful Worksheets to download, up-to-date information,
and bonus content that didn't make it into the book.
Trust me, you don't want to miss this great added value.

It's FREE and really easy!
Visit the link below to get started:

SimpleFunMagic.com/Register

ACKNOWLEDGEMENTS

They say that writing a book is a one-person job.

And in some ways I guess that's true. Most of this book was written between 5 and 7 AM (before I had my first Diet Dr. Pepper) with me sitting in my easy chair in my office all by myself.

Writing a book may be a one-person job, but editing a book is a team sport. At least in my world it is.

Writing a book before you have any caffeine in you is probably not the best idea. Let's just say that some of what I wrote was not very good and needed editing and polishing.

I had a bunch of people who helped me with the editing and polishing, and I want to publicly thank you here and now. Your feedback was invaluable. Yes, sometimes it was hard to take, but your suggestions truly made the book better.

I need to start out by thanking The Dream Team. The Dream Team is the people I work with every day. You all are the best. Your support is invaluable. You keep me going. You have the best ideas. I couldn't do any of the things I do without you. Thank you Kimberly, Danny, Tatjana, Kathleen and Shannon. (Yes, I'm saving Stephanie for later.)

For those of you from the Simple Fun Magic Facebook page, I know I kind of abandoned you in the middle of the project. I'm sorry. I got distracted (yes, I get distracted easily) and never came back, but your suggestions in the early days got things rolling.

To the Launch Team, thank you for your continuing support and help.
I couldn't do this without you. You make me proud of the team we have built.
I really appreciate each of you.

To Courtney, Stefanie, Carolyn, Carol, and Dolores,
Thank you for helping me edit and proof the book. Your honest, thorough
and thoughtful comments were crucial to making **Dad's Simple Fun Magic
Guide to Walt Disney World Planning** the book it is today.
(Yes, it's all your fault.)

Jamie, thank you for Pigment. He's really cute.

I want to say a very special thank you to my number one assistant Stephanie.
Let's see if I can list everything Stephanie does. She is the assistant writer,
the editor, the proofreader, she keeps me on schedule, helps me with outlines,
creates the layout, graphics, Worksheets, eBooks, wrote most of the bonus content,
interfaces with the editing team, and anyone else that needed input.
(I'm sure I left out about 100 things.)

Anything that needed done during the writing process, Stephanie was right there.
Plus she kept the whole business running so I could go off and "write a book."
I say this all the time but never enough, Stephanie you are the best!

Every author thanks his family and that's a tradition
I can't and don't want to break.

My family is awesome.
Mrs. Mom, The Princess, The Man-Child, Prince Charming and The Southern Belle,
you don't complain when I talk about you publically. You let me drag you
to Walt Disney World and try out my crazy schemes. You are even patient
and loving when I work silly hours even when we're "on vacation."
Thank you! I love you all.

And finally, a big thanks to all of you. Thank you for your support. I truly appreciate
you and look forward to helping you with your next trip to Walt Disney World!

WE'RE GOING TO WALT DISNEY WORLD!!!!

CONTENTS

PRELUDE - THE ONE BIG TRUTH

INTRODUCTION

Simple Fun Magic – What to expect in this book

It's all about YOU! – Making this trip your own

If You Don't Have A Plan – Reasons you need to get a PLAN

Paper or Plastic – How to write down your PLAN

The "B" Word – Make a Budget

SECTION SIMPLE - BACK TO SCHOOL

1: No, It's Not Obvious – Why are you going to Walt Disney World?

2: Me, And You, And A… – Who is going with you?

3: Easy or Hard? – When are you going to go?

4: So Much to Do… – What will you to do when you get there?

5: Let's Eat – Where are you going to dine at WDW?

6: Sleepy Time – Where are you going to sleep?

7: Planes, Trains, or Automobiles – How are you going to get there?

8: Making Reservations – A step-by-step guide

SIMPLE INTERLUDE - DAD'S GOLDEN RULE

SECTION FUN - THE PARKS AND MORE

FUN INTERLUDE - LET'S HAVE SOME FUN!

SECTION MAGIC - "PLUSSING" YOUR VACATION

MAGIC INTERLUDE - STOP AND SMELL THE ROSES

AFTERWORD - ONE SIMPLE FACT

PRELUDE
THE ONE BIG TRUTH

"Walt Disney World is a tribute to the philosophy and life of Walter Elias Disney... May Walt Disney World bring joy and inspiration and new knowledge to all who come to this happy place...."
- *Roy O. Disney*, October 25, 1971 (Dedication of Walt Disney World)*

We are going to Walt Disney World.

Those are seven of the scariest words in the whole English language.

Scariest?

Yes, scariest. Let me explain.

If you are going to Walt Disney World, you're probably thinking:

> *"Now what? Where do I start? How am I going to…? Then there's all the inconsistent information. One website says "go left" the next says, "go right." Uncle Johnny says, "you need to…" but Aunt Jane says, "oh no, don't do that!" I'm so confused."*

Or maybe you feel like this…

*Roy O. Disney was Walt Disney's brother, business partner, and co-founder of Walt Disney Productions (which is known today as The Walt Disney Company).

"Oh, my. There's so much to know. So much to do. Which hotel should I pick? What room at that hotel? I saw something about a 5-hour line, are we going to get stuck in line all day? Should we go to the Magic Kingdom first? Epcot? Animal Kingdom? Is there any reason to go to Disney's Hollywood Studios during the construction? Will little Jane be tall enough to ride anything? Do I need a passport? What's a FastPass+? MDE, DME, ADR, DDP, LMNOP what are all of these acronyms?! Can somebody please HELP me? I'm so overwhelmed!"

Yes, I can help. Take a look:

Hi. I'm Carl Trent, but my friends (that includes you!) call me "Dad."

First, right off the bat, I want to make this pledge to you:

You've got a friend in me. I love Walt Disney World. Dad KNOWS Walt Disney World. And I'm here to make your Walt Disney World vacation Simple, Fun, and Magic!

THE ONE BIG TRUTH

We need to start off by talking about the **ONE BIG TRUTH** that you should know about a Walt Disney World vacation.

I got the idea for the **ONE BIG TRUTH** one day at church. I spend a lot of time at church. What can I say? That's who I am.

One Sunday, our boy preacher (OK, he's over 30 but he looks about 14), was talking about some boring topic that I wasn't listening to (not really Phil, I was listening, I'm just saying I wasn't for dramatic effect) when he said something about the one big truth.

What? My ears perked up (no, they don't perk up like a dog, but I started paying attention).

The one big truth. I even wrote it down: "The One Big Truth."

The more I thought about it, the more I was sure that there was one big truth about Walt Disney World. I think it is the reason our family has such great trips when we go.

Are you ready for this?

Are you ready for Dad to share the **ONE BIG TRUTH**?

OK, here we go…

The **ONE BIG TRUTH** is…

Profound, isn't it?

You really need to see this on video to get the full effect:

Now wasn't that Fun?

I'm serious. You are going to Walt Disney World!

That's not something that should be scary.

Going to Walt Disney World is really something special. It's something to be celebrated. It's something to be laughed about. It's something to be shared.

So let's have a party!

Trust me. This is going to be so much Fun!

If you are overwhelmed when you think about a Walt Disney World vacation, if you are confused, if you are a little scared... that's okay!

Relax. Dad is here to help.

A Walt Disney World Vacation is Simple. It's Fun. It's Magic.

You can do this!

We are going to work through this together. Along the way, we're going to make all that confusing, scary stuff about Walt Disney World Simple. I promise, we're going to have a lot of Fun. We're even going to make a little Magic.

Trust me.

You're going to Walt Disney World!!!

The Next Step

In the first step in our journey together, I'll introduce myself properly and tell you what to expect in *Dad's Simple Fun Magic Guide to Walt Disney World Planning*.

SIMPLE, FUN, MAGIC
WHAT TO EXPECT IN THIS BOOK

"Welcome, Foolish Mortals."
- The Haunted Mansion*

Meet Dad

Hi, my name is Carl Trent. You might know me as Dad from Dad's Guide to WDW.com. I am also the founder of WDW Magazine and WDW Discount Club.

Over the last few years, it's been my privilege to help millions of people with their trips to Walt Disney World, and I can't wait to help you with yours.

To really get to know Dad, just head to the link below:

The Haunted Mansion is a spooky and silly dark ride in Liberty Square at Magic Kingdom.

Before we dive into the juicy stuff, I probably ought to tell you what to expect in *Dad's Simple Fun Magic Guide to Walt Disney World Planning*.

This is not your normal Walt Disney World guidebook.

> *Oh, we hadn't figured out that one yet Dad. Thanks for pointing it out, Captain Obvious.*

You're welcome. I'm just that kind of guy.

Meet Pigment

Everyone, meet Pigment.

> *Hi everyone.*

Hi Pigment.

Pigment is my little alter ego. He's that sometimes angel, sometimes devil that sits on my shoulder. He's kind of a pain.

> *Watch it.*

But he's usually right.

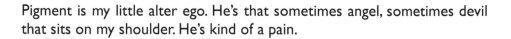

SimpleFunMagic.com/Meet-Pigment

Pigment will pop in from time to time to help keep me on track.

> *Or not.*

Yes, he's been known to distract me…

Where were we?

> *You were talking about Walt Disney World guidebooks…*

Oh, yeah. Thanks, Pigment.

A normal Walt Disney World guidebook is filled with facts and statistics. That's not a bad thing. I love most of the current WDW guidebooks. But this one is a little different.

What To Expect

In *Dad's Simple Fun Magic Guide to Walt Disney World Planning*, I'm going to "teach you how to fish," as the old proverb says. (You know, "Give a man a fish, he eats for a day. Teach a man to fish, he eats for a lifetime." Or something like that.) Another way of saying that is, I'm going to help you plan a Walt Disney World vacation based on your goals and desires.

That is a really big deal. You need to (in the infamous words of Scar*)...

"Be prepared for the chance of a lifetime..."

    Um, I hate to interrupt...

Yes, Pigment... (said in my scariest Scar voice)

Scar is the villain in the 1994 Disney Animated Classic, The Lion King.

Dad, do you remember how that worked out for Scar and his buddies?

You're right, Pigment, It didn't work out so well for them, but the basic idea is still the same.

Simple Fun Magic is all about how, together, we are going take that "chance of a lifetime" and turn it into something you and your family will talk about for the rest of your lives.

In This Book

Dad's Simple Fun Magic Guide to Walt Disney World Planning is divided into four main sections.

The Introduction

There is some foundational information you need to know before we start planning your vacation.

Simple Fun Magic – What to expect in this book

It's all about YOU! – Making this trip your own

If You Don't Have A Plan – Reasons you need to get a PLAN

Paper or Plastic – How to write down your PLAN

The "B" Word – Make a Budget

Once we finish that we can move on to…

Simple – Back to School

A Walt Disney World Vacation is Simple.

There are several Simple questions you will want to answer as you start the planning process.

1: No, It's Not Obvious – Why are you going to Walt Disney World?

2: Me, And You, And A… – Who is going with you?

3: Easy or Hard? – When are you going to go?

4: So Much to Do… – What will you to do when you get there?

Whew. After all those questions it's time for some...

Fun – The Parks and More

Now the Fun begins.

This is where we put together the plan for your Walt Disney World vacation.

But wait, there's more...

Magic – "Plussing" Your Vacation

Let the Magic begin.

There are some things that you can do to get ready for your trip that will really take your vacation to the next level.

22: I've got ADVBS - It's over, what now?

But that's not all.

The Interludes

Sometimes you need a break.

Between each section there is a special chapter that wraps it all up and leads into the next.

> *SIMPLE INTERLUDE - DAD'S GOLDEN RULE*
>
> *FUN INTERLUDE - LET'S HAVE SOME FUN!*
>
> *MAGIC INTERLUDE - STOP AND SMELL THE ROSES*

Trust me, once you get through all of that you will "be prepared for the chance of a lifetime."

> *Hey Dad. I have a few questions. Is this a good time to ask?*

That depends on the question, Pigment, but go ahead.

> *OK, Dad. What's up with these button looking things with links on them I've been seeing? This is a printed book. What are the buttons/links for?*

The Extras

Thank you, Pigment. That's the perfect question.

> *OK, you're welcome, I guess.*

There are so many things that you need to know about your upcoming Walt Disney World vacation, it's impossible to put it all in one book. Many have tried, none have succeeded.

I thought we would sprinkle in a little Magic by adding links to **bonus** content such as videos, helpful tips, charts, lists and things that we just don't have room to talk about in here.

Bonus content like…

- **Videos** – I like music. I sing a lot. I thought it would be Fun to link to the videos from my favorite songs (that make a point) or helpful and Fun videos that catch my eye.

- **Planning tools** – I have developed some nifty planning tools and I have them all ready for you when you click on the buttons.

- **Extra Information** – There's no way to fit everything that I want to say in a book, it would be 6,000 pages long (or more), so there will be a lot of bonus content on the website.

I've also taken all the information about Walt Disney World that could change and put it on the website. Believe or not, things change at WDW:

! SimpleFunMagic.com/Updates

So when you see a button/link, enter the link into a device (computer, tablet, phone) and you'll be taken to the **bonus** content.

Or… If you registered your book at SimpleFunMagic.com/Register, go over to the website (SimpleFunMagic.com) and login. You'll be taken to a homepage where you will see the buttons/links for each chapter. As you're reading, just click on the button and the **bonus** content will pop right up.

Grab your tablet, phone, or laptop… It's Simple, Fun, Magic!

Next question.

Why do you keep capitalizing the words "Simple, Fun and Magic?"

That's a good question, and this is a really good time to answer it.

One of the things I do is use capitalization and punctuation to emphasize things. That's why you see the words Simple, Fun, Magic (and others) capitalized.

Because, as I said in the Prelude…

A Walt Disney World Vacation is Simple. It's Fun. It's Magic.

You should probably make that into a T-Shirt somehow.

Actually, we did Pigment. And a bunch of others, too!

Any other questions?

Not right now. I'll let you know if I think of any.

I'm sure you will.

At the end of every chapter you'll see **Dad's Bottom Line**. It's where I sum up what the chapter is all about, and then **The Next Step** will introduce the upcoming chapter.

Dad's Bottom Line

Dad's Simple Fun Magic Guide to Walt Disney World Planning will prepare you for the chance of a lifetime. The chance for a Simple, Fun, Magic Walt Disney World vacation.

Don't miss out on the bonus content. It's really, really good.

Trust me!

What are you waiting for?

The Next Step

The first thing that we are going to do is to talk about you. Yes, you...

I like talking about me!

I'm sure you do, Pigment. I'm sure you do.

IT'S ALL ABOUT YOU!
MAKING THIS TRIP YOUR OWN

"Paging Mr. Morrow. Mr. Tom Morrow."
- Tomorrowland Transit Authority PeopleMover*

A Short Interruption

We interrupt this program to bring you a special announcement.

Uh, Dad...This is not a TV program. What are you doing?

I am employing what might be called an
attention-getting device.

Do you think it worked?

Why yes, I think it did.

This might be a good time to remind you that
you are going to hear lots and lots of opinions on
what to do on your Walt Disney World vacation.

*Tomorrowland Transit Authority PeopleMover is a slow-moving elevated, tram ride that takes
guests on a tour above Tomorrowland at Magic Kingdom.*

Some of them are going to be very passionate. Don't fall for them.

Remember, YOU are the one going to Walt Disney World. This is YOUR PLAN! What's **THE ONE BIG TRUTH?**

I can't emphasize this enough. YOUR PLAN doesn't have to be perfect. It won't be, it can't be. Nothing is ever perfect. No PLAN survives the first rain shower, or the first bus being late, or the first big tour group with 100 screaming teens. There's always something that messes things up.

That's OK. Relax and enjoy. You will be at the Most Magical Place on Earth.

Repeat after me. Ready?

"This is my PLAN. I will do what I want."

> *"This is Dad's PLAN. I will do what he wants."*

Wait a minute, it's not "This is Dad's PLAN. I'll do what he wants." This is YOUR PLAN. You are going to do what YOU want.

> *My plan. Like me, Pigment? This is MY plan?!*

Now you're getting it.

So let's try that again. Repeat after me:

"This is my PLAN. I will do what I want."
"This is my PLAN. I will do what I want."
"This is my PLAN. I will do what I want."

> *"This is my PLAN. I will do what I want."*
> *"This is my PLAN. I will do what I want."*
> *"This is my PLAN. I will do what I want."*
>
> *Hey, Dad. This is Fun!*

OK, I think we are ready to move on.

I know you have seen this: a Walt Disney World commercial comes on the TV. A beautiful mom, a dad with a million dollar (fake) smile, two and a half perfect children, with the little girl holding a Mickey Mouse balloon scampering down Main Street toward Cinderella Castle.

It's a clear, blue-sky day, there are only 20 people in the park and everything is perfect. And you just know they booked Fido into Best Friends Pet Care* for an incredible day of pampering. Oh, what a beautiful day!

SimpleFunMagic.com/Oh-What-A-Beautiful-Morning

NEWS FLASH: You are not that beautiful family.
Your Walt Disney World experience will be somewhat different from that.

> *Oh, Dad! Why are you dissing these nice people? What on earth are you talking about? Those people in the video are perfect. Why can't every family have a perfect Walt Disney World experience?*

Let me explain.

Best Friends Pet Care is essentially a pet hotel on Disney property where your furry friends can relax and have Fun while you're enjoying all that WDW has to offer.

I wish you would…

OK, I'll try.

Reality Check

You are not that beautiful family in the commercial. That beautiful family is not real. They are fictional. They are actors. The whole thing is staged complete with makeup, special lighting, crowd control, painted on smiles, etc. It probably took them several hours just to shoot a 3-second scene.

That commercial is not reality. It's a dream.

You aren't that family.

You are different.

> *Will you quit saying that? I know I'm different, but usually nice people don't mention it.*

Now, wait a minute. That's not what I'm saying at all. You are different. I am different *(you got that right)*. We are all different. And that's good. There's no one I'd rather be than me.

SimpleFunMagic.com/Bad-Guy-Affirmation

Poor Ralph*.

On January 20, 1992, *Time Magazine* had a cover story that proclaimed (this is a paraphrase so don't jump on me): Men and women are different and they might be born that way.

Did you know that?

Men and women are different.

Ralph is the main character in the 2012 Disney Animated Classic, Wreck-It Ralph.

Yes, *Time Magazine* got it wrong, wrong, wrong.

Not only are men and women different, EVERYONE is different. No two people are exactly the same.

I have identical twin cousins. From the very beginning these guys looked almost exactly alike. Even their own father couldn't tell them apart.

They were raised in the same house. Inseparable. They were always dressed exactly alike (yes, they had to dress alike). They ate the same foods, were in the same classes in school, everything in their lives was identical.

But they aren't the same. They are different. One is a preacher and the other is a computer salesman. One married a quiet blonde. The other married an outspoken brunette. They don't think alike. They don't act alike.

They still look somewhat alike. People will come up to one and think he is the other, but they are different.

We all are. That is a good thing!

Yes, it's a good thing. Think about it. What if everyone was EXACTLY like you? Or even worse, what if everyone was EXACTLY like ME? Yuck. The world would be a pretty boring place.

NO, I AM NOT BORING!

Think about it. If everyone was just like me, most of the restaurants in the world would be gone. There wouldn't be any romance novels. Sports would be pretty boring because everyone would be cheering for the same teams.

We are all different.

> OK Dad, you've beaten that dead horse long enough. So what? We are different. Get to the point.

Good idea, Pigment. Here's the point:

It's YOUR Vacation

YOU are going to Walt Disney World. YOUR vacation is not going to be like anyone else's Walt Disney World Vacation.

Let me say that again.

What you experience at Walt Disney World will be different than what your neighbor, your friend, some random person on the Internet or book writer will experience.

So let me ask you one big favor as we move forward: tune out the world. Don't go looking around on the Internet for other opinions. When Uncle Jimmy or Aunt Sally try to tell you what you "have to do," just don't listen. Just set your Mickey ears to KDAD and let's get you ready for the chance of a lifetime.

> **LISTEN TO DAD. TRUST DAD. LISTEN TO DAD. TRUST DAD.**
> **LISTEN TO DAD. TRUST DAD. LISTEN TO DAD. TRUST DAD.**
> **LISTEN TO DAD. TRUST DAD. LISTEN TO DAD. TRUST DAD.**
> **LISTEN TO DAD. TRUST DAD. LISTEN TO DAD. TRUST DAD.**
> **LISTEN TO DAD. TRUST DAD. LISTEN TO DAD. TRUST DAD.**

Good. Let's go!

Dad's Bottom Line

We are all different and that's a GREAT thing. So for the rest of this book we are going to talk about how to celebrate YOU. How to create a Simple PLAN for your WaltDisney World trip so you can have Fun as you experience the Most Magical Place on Earth!

The Next Step

Next up, we are going to talk about the foundation of a PLAN, including the One, Single, Big Secret Thing.

> *Oooh! That sounds cool!*

It is, Pigment. It is.

IF YOU DON'T HAVE A PLAN
REASONS YOU NEED TO GET A PLAN

**"You are about to discover what lies beyond the Fifth Dimension. Beyond the deepest, darkest corner of your imagination...
in the Tower of Terror."
- The Twilight Zone Tower of Terror***

Back when I was growing up there was a commercial on TV for the Western Company that said, "If you don't have an oil well... get one!"

If we change it up a bit, that's a perfect saying for Walt Disney World. If you don't have a Walt Disney World PLAN, get one!

A while ago, I was reading posts in a Facebook group when a lady posted a story about her recent Walt Disney World experience.

Her family went on a one-day trip to WDW. They were going to the Magic Kingdom. They arrived at 11am. She was upset because they were only able to ride five rides before they left at dinnertime. She complained that she didn't even find out about FastPass+ until late in the afternoon. They had spent over $300 and didn't feel the Magic.

Dad, that's so sad.

*The Twilight Zone Tower of Terror is a thrill ride that can be found on Sunset Boulevard at Disney's Hollywood Studios.

Yes it is Pigment. This poor family came unprepared. They didn't have a PLAN, and they didn't have any Fun.

> *Is there any way I can be sure that doesn't happen to me?*

Yes there is. This is what *Dad's Simple Fun Magic Guide to Walt Disney World Planning* is all about. Working to develop the "perfect" PLAN for YOU!

You know, there's an old Carly Simon song that talks about Dad and Walt Disney World planning. Check it out:

 SimpleFunMagic.com/Nobody-Does-It-Better

Oh, Carly, thank you, you are so right, but no, I am not "so vain" (…but you ARE always singing about me).

This is going to be Fun.

One, Single, Big, Secret Thing

There is one thing. One single thing. One single, big thing. One single, big, secret thing. There is One, Single, Big, Secret Thing which - more than anything else - will ensure that you have a stress-free Walt Disney World Vacation.

I want to tell you a little story. This is what happened the first time I actually tried to make a plan for the family.

This was written about a trip in 1994 – things were different then! Some of the attractions that I mention in this tale no longer exist. Don't worry – lots of great new stuff is open now that wasn't then.

Titanic has nothing on me…

THE PLAN was perfect…

Books will be written about **THE PLAN**...

Monuments will be built to **THE PLAN**...

Hundreds of hours had gone in to developing **THE PLAN**...

Years of research went in to **THE PLAN**...

THE PLAN was going perfectly...

Until...

~ Late May, 1994 ~

It was one of those perfect Florida late spring mornings. The sun broke over the horizon and danced lightly on the perfectly manicured, dew-covered lawn. Birds (real ones) sang softly from the abundant foliage. The early morning colors exploded trumpeting the start to another lovely day.

THE PLAN was succeeding beyond my wildest dreams. We had stopped at the Disney Travel Center in Ocala on our way down and found a great price for upgrading to the Polynesian Village Resort. When we checked in they gave us a room in the Pago Pago building. Perfect! We were less than 100 yards from the Ticket and Transportation Center and the Monorail.

When the alarms went off that morning, the kids jumped right out of bed. They were so excited. The Man-Child absolutely loved the day bed. He thought it was put in the room just for him. He already had a nest built. The Princess got to sleep in a bed all by herself. She was pumped. She got both of their autograph books packed and ready to go (what a good sister!).

THE PLAN was working brilliantly. The girls brought over breakfast while the boys got ready. We walked out of the room, over to the Epcot Monorail platform at the Transportation and Ticket Center.

We were the only ones there, so we asked to ride with the driver and they said yes (oh boy, those were the days – that doesn't happen anymore!). It was awesome.

We jumped off the Monorail and ran right over to the Living Seas. **THE PLAN** called for getting the Living Seas done and then rushing across the park to Body Wars.

It was perfect. There was no line. We walked right on to the Hydrolator. (Did you know those things only moved 2 inches? I'd have swore it was at least 10 feet.)

The Man-Child loves fishies. He could have spent all day gazing at the aquariums in the Living Seas, but **THE PLAN** said it was time to move on.

We came out of the Living Seas and I started to rush us over to Body Wars when IT happened.

"Why can't we go into that building? It looks like Fun!" someone said innocently.

BOOOOOOOOOOMMMMMMMMMM

"Because it's not on **THE PLAN**," I said forcefully (being the Dad, and leader of the family, whenever I say something forcefully that's all that needs to be said).

"What Plan?" Mrs. Mom asked.

FFFFFLLLLLLLUUUUUUUUSSSSSSSSHHHHHHHHHH

"**THE PLAN!**" I said boldly. (It was time to put an end to this uprising and get back on **THE PLAN**.)

"Where did this plan come from?" she asked.

CCCCCCRRRRRRRRRRRAAAAAAAAAASSSSSSSSSHHHHHH

"**THE PLAN**, it came from above." I said trying to put a humorous end to this useless bickering and get back on schedule.

We were now 5 minutes behind on **THE PLAN**.

"I'd like to see this plan." She said.

DDDOOOWWWNNN IIINNN FFFLLLAAAMMMEEESSS

It was time to put an end to this. We were rapidly loosing time and lines were getting longer each second. It was time to put my foot down.

"NO. We've got to get moving or we won't get everything done," I said. (You should have been there, I was such a MAN.)

Mrs. Mom was not having it and said, "Come on kids, let's go back to the hotel, your dad's being unreasonable, again." (What do you mean again? I'm the most reasonable man you'll ever know.)

Moral of the Story

THE PLAN was a thing of beauty, and once I shared it with the family and got everyone on board, THE PLAN worked perfectly.

I had spent hours researching and developing a plan. The only problem was I didn't take time to let the family help develop it.

We sat down that night and went over **THE PLAN** for each day. Everyone made suggestions, and we improved on **THE PLAN**. Once we all agreed, The New Plan was great. The trip was great. We had a blast.

Great story Dad! But what's the point?

Here's the point: the One, Single, Big Secret Thing that more than anything else will help you have a Stress Free Walt Disney World Vacation is…

You guessed it. You Need A PLAN.

It sounds so Simple doesn't it?

The One, Single, Big Secret Thing that will let you have a stress-free WDW Vacation is: A PLAN.

> *But Dad, I don't make plans. I just go with the flow.*

Oooh, oooh, I do love that song…

(Dad sounds a lot like that cool Crush* guy when he sings. Dad sings good.)

Really, Pigment? No plan?

When you go on vacation, do you get up whenever you feel like it, just hop in the car, and go with the flow of traffic? No direction in mind? You'll just know where you're going when you get there?

Going to Walt Disney World with the idea that you are just going to go with the flow is nothing short of INSANE!

Not all PLANS are created equal

> *But Dad, Dude, PLANS are so confining. There's no spontaneity.*
> *Every minute it will feel like we have to run to the next ride. I hate PLANS.*
> *I'm a free spirit. I like to roll with the punches.*
> *Yes, I still want to go with the flow…*

That's OK Pigment, going with the flow is one way to do things. I can't say I understand going with the flow, I like having structure. But remember, we are all different. That's a good thing. The same is true when it comes to planning. All PLANS are different. Even plans that go with the flow.

This one is just right…

Planning a trip to Walt Disney World is kind of like the story of Goldilocks. Everyone has their own preferences on how detailed their PLAN should be.

Crush is a character in the 2003 Pixar film Finding Nemo. At WDW, you can see him at Animal Kingdom in Finding Nemo – The Musical or at Epcot in Turtle Talk with Crush.

For some, a PLAN needs to have every minute of their trip mapped out (hot). For others, a moderately detailed PLAN (warm) with a bit of wiggle room works. Then there is the bare outline – the go with the flow type of a PLAN (cold) – but it's still a PLAN!

You have to pick the level of PLAN that's "just right" for your family. Are you the hot, warm, or cold planners?

Planning is not a Solo Sport

The other big takeaway from Dad's planning debacle is that planning is not a Solo Sport.

Everyone who is going on the trip should be involved in the planning process. Just look at what happened when I tried to make a PLAN without involving the whole family. It was a nightmare.

As we go through the book there are going to be a lot of opportunities to share parts of your PLAN with your traveling companions. Each of the planning chapters have downloadable Worksheets that are meant to be shared.

Dad's Bottom Line

The One, Single, Big Secret Thing you need to know about a Walt Disney World vacation is it will be better with A PLAN!

And you should share each stage of your plan with your traveling companions because planning is not a Solo Sport.

Some sort of shared plan is essential for a Simple, Fun, Magic Walt Disney World vacation!

The Next Step

We are almost ready to start making your PLAN, but there are a couple more things that we have to do before we get into the details. The next step is to talk about writing down your PLAN on paper.

I have to write it down? What Fun is that?!

Yes Pigment, you have to write it down!

PAPER OR PLASTIC
HOW TO WRITE DOWN YOUR PLAN

"Remember how easy it was to learn your ABC's?
Thank the Phoenicians, they invented them."
– Spaceship Earth*

Paper or Plastic? Which are you?

Is this some Guardians of the Galaxy** question?

OK, you stumped me on that one Pigment, why are you talking about *Guardians of the Galaxy?*

You know, when Drax says, "I think of Sakaaran people as paper people?"
Is this Paper vs. Plastic thing something like that? A galactic death match?

No, Pigment! It's not like that at all (but I do love the music from those movies). It's more like when you go to the grocery store and the checkout clerk asks you, "Paper or Plastic?"

You have a choice. Which do you choose? Some choose Paper, some choose Plastic. No, we're not going to talk about those who bring their own bags.

---

*Spaceship Earth is the iconic "golf ball" of Epcot and it houses a great attraction that explains human progress through the ages. **Guardians of the Galaxy is a film franchise produced by Disney, based on the Marvel comic of the same name.

Or maybe a better question would be: are you Technology or are you Old School?

When it comes to planning the vacation of a lifetime, are you Plastic and Technology, or maybe, Paper and Old School?

> *I think I'm beginning to understand. It's kind of like you and Mrs. Mom when you plan your vacations. Right?*

Now you're on the right track, Pigment.

Paper vs. Plastic

When it's time to start planning a trip to Walt Disney World, a very interesting thing happens around our house. Right after Mrs. Mom and I say those fateful words:

"We're going to Walt Disney World!"

I go to my office, and Mrs. Mom heads to her office and we start planning our vacation.

For me, out comes the laptop, iPad and iPhone. I start diving into Touringplans.com, My Disney Experience, Dad's Guide to WDW, WDW Magazine, WDW Discount Club, the official Walt Disney World website, and about a thousand more online tools. Plastic, Technology... that's me.

Mrs. Mom loads up a bunch of paper into her printer and starts printing out piles of stuff. Menus, calendars, schedules... Paper, Old School... that's Mrs. Mom.

Then she starts building the "trip bible."

Mrs. Mom's "trip bible" has every detail that we will need for the whole trip, right in one place.

The "trip bible" is so cool that we're going to discuss it more in just a minute.

On our evening walks we'll discuss every detail of the trip. I'm not kidding! Every night for months, we'll talk about Walt Disney World during these strolls. It's the best time of the day.

It's during our walks that the PLAN starts to come together. Mrs. Mom will print out information and put it in the "trip bible" and I'll log it into my devices and set up the electronic tracking.

Finally, when the big day comes, I grab my iPhone, iPad, laptop and brain (don't want to forget the brain), and Mrs. Mom grabs her "trip bible." And off we go.

Paper and Plastic. Technology and Old School. Together at last.

It works.

Mrs. Mom's "trip bible"

Let's start by looking at Mrs. Mom's "trip bible."
Yes, "bible" with a little "b."

Dad, isn't calling it a "bible" a little sacrilegious?

I hope not. That's why I use the little "b." The name "bible" came from the fact that, as it evolved, Mrs. Mom's "trip bible" seemed to have as many pages as the real Bible. We treat it with roughly as much reverence and it's almost as important. We definitely mean no disrespect to the real thing with our little nickname.

You're going to want to create your own "trip bible" – or whatever you want to call it.

Mrs. Mom's "trip bible" has EVERYTHING. Every piece of paper that we could possibly need for the trip.

In just a few seconds, Mrs. Mom can whip out a reservation number or a menu on the spot. It really comes in handy.

The frustrating thing is that she always beats me when I try to pull things up on my app…

So, would you like to know what's in Mrs. Mom's "trip bible"?

Mrs. Mom's "trip bible" has:

- Travel Information:
    - Airline
    - Hotels
    - Rental Car
    - Tickets
    - Special Events
- Restaurant Menus:
    - Table Service
    - Quick Service
    - Airport Restaurants
- Advanced Dining Reservation confirmation numbers
- Passports (and other important documents)
- Park hours calendar
- Daily Itinerary Cards
- The appropriate Get Down to Disness Daily Agenda* pages
- The PLAN

The "trip bible" is all very organized. It's broken up into days. Each day has it's own plastic sleeve with the papers for that day. Each morning we grab the sleeve for the day, throw it in the backpack, and we're off.

We know a lot of people that do something similar. Or something totally different. Check out these examples of different "trip bibles" from Dad's friends:

While I'm a big techie, there really is a place for Paper when you're planning a WDW vacation.

You need Technology too...

In 2008, Disney began working on a revolutionary new concept. The project

*The Get Down to Disness Daily Agenda is a favorite planning tool of ours to help keep track of our daily PLAN. Head on over to the link above to learn more about it!

was code named "Next Generation Experience" or "NextGen." The idea was to incorporate technology into EVERYTHING at the Disney Parks and enhance the Guest experience.

This is probably the biggest project Disney has ever taken on. Over two billion dollars has been poured into NextGen.

In 2013, the name was changed to MyMagic+, and, in case you think that this is a passing fad, in 2015, Bob Iger (the CEO of the Walt Disney Company), told his senior staff to "fall in love with technology."

Today, every aspect of a Walt Disney World vacation has a MyMagic+ component. Even going to the bathroom (yep – maps to the nearest restroom are incorporated into live maps) is part of the program.

It all starts with My Disney Experience

What is My Disney Experience and why should I care? I'm a Paper pig. I'm not ever going to use that techy stuff. It scares me.

Silly Pigment. Check out this video from Disney –

OK, that's a little extreme, but… You will definitely want to get familiar with it, because My Disney Experience is EVERYWHERE at Walt Disney World.

Just how pervasive is it? You can't get into your Disney hotel room, into a park, eat at a sit down restaurant, use the Disney Dining Plan, or get a FastPass+ without My Disney Experience and the technology behind it.

It takes your picture, it shows you where to go, it keeps track of EVERYTHING.

Takes my picture? Where? You know I'm camera shy. Can't order a meal? Can't open my hotel room door? CAN'T GET INTO THE PARK!? Maybe I just won't go to WDW!

Whoa, Nellie! Whoa! Or should I say: Whoa, Pigment, Whoa! Settle down. It's going to be OK. Take a deep breath. Dad's here. Relax. Trust me...

It's going to be alright.

Feeling better?

Oh, yeah. I'm a movin' slow, so it's alright... Oh, it's alright...

That's great Pigment. Isn't Dad helpful?

Do I have to answer that?

That hurt.

Speaking of being helpful...

The first thing that you are going to do as you start your Plastic/Technology experience is to set up MDE.

MDE? Are we using abbreviations now?!

Good point, Pigment. I'm not really a fan of abbreviations or acronymns, but they are pretty pervasive in Disney jargon. I'll try not to use them too much in this book, but you're bound to come across some in your research. I've put together a reference guide to help you out:

Relax, it's pretty Simple. I've put together a real easy video that will show you how to set up your my Disney Experience Account.

Aren't I a nice guy? Hush Pigment...

Really, for the most part, My Disney Experience is Simple. It can be a lot of Fun. It is actually powered by Magic.

Disney even takes all the information in your my Disney Experience account and through some neat computer technology sends it to a wrist band you'll wear throughout your trip (called a MagicBand).

Everything we talked about earlier (getting into your hotel room, dining reservations, the Disney Dining Plan, FastPass+, park tickets) and more is all on your MagicBand.

> *Wow Dad! Did the Imagineers* coat the computers with Pixie Dust** or something?*

Maybe, Pigment. Maybe.

A marriage made in Disney heaven

When it comes to a Walt Disney World vacation the Paper versus Plastic, Technology vs. Old School contrast is like Dad and Mrs. Mom. A marriage made in Disney heaven.

> *Ah, Dad that's so cute. Did you make that up yourself or have some help from Mrs. Mom?*

Oh, that's all me Pigment. Dad, the romantic.

Dad's Simple Fun Magic Guide to Walt Disney World Planning is about creating the PLAN for your "chance of a lifetime" vacation. We are going to do that together by marrying Paper and Plastic, Technology and Old School.

Throughout the rest of the book, we'll be setting up your My Disney Experience app and creating your very own "trip bible." In each section there will be Worksheets, lists, maps, and instructions on how to set up the My Disney Experience app.

---

*Imagineers is the term Disney uses to refer to their team members who work on research and development for new concepts and technologies in the parks. **Pixie Dust is what Peter Pan uses to fly (courtesy of his friend, Tinkerbell) in the 1953 Disney Animated Classic of the same name. It's also a commonly used term among Disney fans for adding special touches to your vacation.

In the last section I'll have what I call a "Final Exam" where we'll check your "trip bible" and compare it to your My Disney Experience account to be sure you're all ready to go.

Dad's Bottom Line

You have to have Dad and Mrs. Mom, BOTH Paper and Plastic, BOTH Technology and Old School for your PLAN to be successful.

Yes, you have to have both. Don't worry. We'll work on it together.

The Next Step

The next step is to work through our first Paper vs. Plastic experience. We're going to talk about the… I think I'll surprise you with the topic.

Dad, remember, we don't like surprises.

You're right, Pigment. You're right.

THE "B" WORD
MAKE A BUDGET

"I am not your mother – break those plates!"
- Toy Story Mania*

When you start to PLAN a Walt Disney World vacation you should begin with the dreaded "B" word: budget.

This is going to be Fun.

Um, Dad. I'm not so sure that talking about the "B" word is all that Fun if you get my drift.

Oh, I totally agree with you Pigment. I hate the "B" word.

You, agree with me? Will wonders never cease?

I am terrible at budgetting. I've always been terrible with budgets.

*Toy Story Mania is an interactive video game and dark ride hybrid in Pixar Place at Disney's Hollywood Studios.

I am one of those math guys (I love playing with numbers) who can't make a budget. I'm not wired that way. (I said wired, not weird, same letters, different meaning. Very different meaning.)

> *Uh, Dad, you're not good with budgets, but you are going to try to teach us to budget? Huh? Not getting a really positive vibe here.*

Trust me, Pigment. I may not be very good at budgeting, but I am pretty good at making things Fun. Besides, this is the foundation of your PLAN.

> *OK, Dad, if you say so...*

I do.

You need a budget

Now it's time to make a budget for your Walt Disney World Vacation. Yes, I know. You hate making budgets. I hate making budgets. Everyone hates budgets, except for accountants, right? It's time to learn to love the budget.

Making a budget is extremely important for any vacation. There's nothing that can take away the Magic of Disney faster than having money problems during a trip.

This is the most important chapter in the book. Trust me. Talking about money is something that – if you're like me – you try to avoid, but is really the first thing that you need to do when you are planning a trip to Walt Disney World.

Let's see if we can't add an element of Fun. Let's try to make it Simple. Who knows? We might even stumble into a little Magic.

Money struggles

One of the worst things that can happen to you at Walt Disney World is to have money struggles. It can ruin the Fun really quickly. We saw how this can affect a trip when we were at Walt Disney World in 2012.

We were having breakfast at Pepper Market in the Coronado Springs Resort, when we noticed a young couple sitting at a table. Yep, I'm a highly trained observer and I notice things.

Big deal Dad, you noticed a young couple.

OK, that's not all that unusual, but this young couple was obviously having some difficulties. They were looking at their hotel bill and it was clear that it wasn't a happy conversation.

> The bill was like 100 pages long. OK 100 might be an exaggeration, but it was huge. It was at least 30 pages.
>
> The couple was going through the bill, page-by-page, and talking about each one. The wife would point at something and an animated conversation would ensue.
>
> Then they would settle that one and move on to the next. More animated conversation. This went on the whole time we were eating. They were still having this "conversation" when we left.
>
> We went back to the hotel room, brushed our teeth and came back to grab a last minute drink before hopping on the bus and they were still going at it another twenty minutes later.
>
> They weren't having a lot of Fun.

My guess is that they could have avoided a lot of heartache and "animated conversation" if they would have just started with the "B" word.

Making a budget is something big. It affects everyone in the family and it should be discussed by everyone in the family, especially the adults.

Remember, planning a Walt Disney World vacation is not a Solo Sport!

How much can we afford?

When we talk about Walt Disney World, the first question I'm always thinking about is how much does it cost?

SimpleFunMagic.com/How-Much-Does-It-Cost

Starting with, "How much does it cost?" is the wrong attitude. It will get you into a bunch of problems. Trust me.

A better question is, "How much can we afford?"

Let's dive into that.

Do you have a family budget? I sure hope so.

If you do have a family budget this is going to be easy. What amount in your family budget is allotted for a vacation? Done. That's what your Walt Disney World budget is.

Dad is good.

> *I don't need a budget, Dad. I've got a credit card. I'll just put the whole trip on my credit card and not worry about it. It's the American way.*

No, Pigment! Or as Queen says:

SimpleFunMagic.com/no-no-no-no-no-no-no

Debt is Dumb

Dave Ramsey* is well know for saying Debt is Dumb. Dave is exactly right. Debt is Dumb.

The stup…

> *Dad you told me to tell you when you are about to say a bad word. That's a bad word.*

Bad word? Hockey puck! Stupi….

> *Dad. Stop. Try a different word, please.*

OK, how about this: the silliest thing you can do is put your vacation on a credit card and pay it off over time. It's just nuts.

Dave Ramsey is a radio talk show host who talks about a disciplined approach to household finances, including a strict management of debt.

Let's do some quick math. The average credit card interest, these days, is around 17%. If you were to put a $3,000 trip on your credit card, how long would it take to pay it off?

- At $100 per month, it would take 3 years and 2 months, and you would pay $800 dollars extra in interest.
- At $75 per month, it would take almost 5 years, and you'd pay $1,425 in interest.
- At $50 per month, it would take almost 11 years, and you'd pay $8,500 in interest - more than double the original amount!

Yikes. It's no wonder credit card companies are some of the most profitable in the world.

Can we agree that the credit card thing isn't an option? I hope so.

OK Dad, no credit cards. I get it. We still want to go to Walt Disney World. We don't have a budget, what can we do?

That's a very good question. Let's see if I can answer it.

- First you need to make a budget.
- Put a line item in your budget for vacations.
- Take the vacation money and put in a safe place where you won't spend it on pizza or something.
- When you've saved up enough you get to go to Walt Disney World!

It's so Simple, yet so hard.

Uh, Dad. I don't have a budget, so what do I do?

Didn't I just answer that, Pigment? You make one!

Can I get a little help with that?

I think we can arrange that, Pigment. In fact, I've put together a pretty amazing budget spreadsheet to give you that help. It will help you create both a household budget plus a trip budget.

 SimpleFunMagic.com/Little-Help

How's that for a little help?

> *So now I have my budget. Can I ask a silly question? I'm setting aside a certain amount every payday for my WDW vacation. But where am I supposed to put it so I won't spend it on something else?*

Pigment, you are on a roll with the good questions today.

> *Thank you!*

This will sound crazy, but send it to Disney.

> *And just how am I supposed to do that?*

And the hits just keep on rolling. It's like you are in my head Pigment.

Make payments on your reservation

The Simple way to send money to Disney is to make payments on your reservation. Here's how it works:

1 - You make a reservation for a room or package.
2 - You make a down payment on the reservation.
3 - You make payments until your reservation is paid off.
4 - Then it's time for Dad's **One Big Truth**:

Saving spending money

You might be looking for ways to save "spending money" for your trip. That's a great idea.

Mrs. Mom cuts coupons for the groceries. She pays full price and gets the coupon money for change. She takes the coupon money, puts it in a big cup, and hides it from Dad (I'm the spender in the family).

When it's time to go on vacation, Mrs. Mom pulls out the vacation cup, and we have a ton of spending money. It's usually about $1,000 per year and pays for most of our food and souvenirs.

I know that there are a lot of people who give up something, and take that money and use it for vacations. Let's say you go to Starbucks every morning and pay $5 for a cup of coffee (Dad is not a coffee drinker so I'm making this up).

Buy coffee and make it at home instead of going to Starbucks. Take that $5 per day and put it away for the trip. In less than a year, you will have saved $1,000. Easy peasy.

Yes, I know you need your Starbucks, but you can pick something else. The point is to find a way to save $5 a day and you'll pay for a third of your trip in under a year!

> *Dad, I know you're not the Starbucks type, but your friend Stephanie suggested that they could switch to brewed coffee from a latte or get a smaller size, and save $2 a day.*

Stephanie is very smart Pigment. Every little bit counts.

How much does it cost

> *Now that we have a budget, can I finally look to see how much it costs to go to Walt Disney World?*

Yes, Pigment, now is a good time to look at the prices for your trip, but just to look. We'll talk about making reservations and stuff later.

Just head on over to disneyworld.com, fill out the "Price Your Vacation" form at the top of the page and see how much your trip might cost. I'll wait…

…Oh! You're back! Nice to see you again.

So, here's a question for you, what did you think when you looked?

Disney Sticker Shock

Wait, let me guess. I bet you were shocked, right?

Wow. How did you know that? This is getting scary.

Want to know my secret? I have Magical powers. I watched *The Flash* so many times that I've absorbed enough particle accelerator explosions to have metahuman powers of my own.

My metahuman power is to KNOW. Dad KNOWS Disney and I KNOW what YOU are thinking. It's a gift.

Oh, and every time I look at Disney's prices, I'm shocked, and so is everyone else I know, so I figured that you probably would be too. I call it Disney Sticker Shock.

I'm not going to get into a big boring history lesson about prices, or argue about whether a Disney Vacation is worth the money but I will acknowledge the fact that it can be very expensive to go to Walt Disney World.

Poly tastes on a Pop budget

When I start looking at prices and dreaming of a WDW trip, the first thing I look at is the price of Disney's Polynesian Village Resort. I love that Resort. It's my favorite spot, in my favorite place, in the whole wide world.

Disney's Polynesian Village Resort (which I like to call the Poly for short) is the one over by the Magic Kingdom that looks like it could have been shipped in right off the beaches of Oahu. It's beautiful inside and out.

It's what Disney calls a Deluxe Resort, meaning that it's one of the highest priced hotels on the property. A "cheap" room at the Poly costs around $600 per night. That's out of my price range.

If I were to win the lottery, I'd probably buy about a bazillion Disney Vacation Club* points at Disney's Polynesian Village and live there year round. In a Bora Bora Bungalow right on the water. Wouldn't that be cool?

That's my dream.

SimpleFunMagic.com/The-Polynesian-Village-Resort

But it's not my reality. My reality usually is that I can only afford to stay at Disney's Pop Century Resort. That's what the budget allows.

Don't get me wrong, I love the Pop (my pet name for Disney's Pop Century Resort).

The Pop is a cool looking hotel with all bright colors and big icons from a bunch of different decades. Icons like a Big Wheel, a Rubik's Cube, or a 60-foot tall jar of Play Dough. There's even a huge 8-Track tape in one of the sections.

The Pop is the hotel with the most rooms at WDW. It has over 2,800 rooms (2,884 to be exact). It's one of the Value Resorts, which are the least expensive hotels at Disney World.

SimpleFunMagic.com/Tour-Of-The-Pop

I love the Pop, it's my home away from home. For the last fifteen years or so, we've stayed at the Pop more than any other Resort. In fact, more than all of the others combined. But, I still dream of the Poly.

When it comes to Disney vacations, I have Poly tastes on a Pop budget!

Hey Dad, what's your point?

Disney Vacation Club is Disney's timeshare program.

Sometimes we have to compromise. What we want, or what we dream of, the fantasy may not be what we can afford. And that's OK!

Maybe you can't afford to stay at the most expensive hotels. That's OK. Maybe you can't afford to stay in a Disney hotel. That's OK. Maybe you have to stay fifteen miles away. That's OK too!

This is YOUR vacation.

You are in charge and remember the **ONE BIG TRUTH:**

That's big. That's important. It doesn't matter if you only spent $35 per night on your hotel. In fact, that may make you the smartest person in the whole place.

Dad's Bottom Line

It's crucial, critical, essential, vital, imperative, important, and every other word for "necessary" in the thesaurus, that you have a budget.

Once you have a budget you'll know what you can spend on your Walt Disney World vacation, and how long it will take you to save up. You might have to make choices, like Dad does between the Poly and the Pop. But that's OK.

The Next Step

It's time to go back to school. No, I'm not kidding.
We are going back to school to English class.
And it will be Fun!

> *English Class? I thought you didn't like*
> *English Class.*

I didn't, Pigment. I really didn't.

SIMPLE

And now what you've all been waiting for. It's time to get to work. This is going to be Fun. We're going to go "back to school." Sing it Rod…

🎵 SimpleFunMagic.com/Back-To-School

(Did you sing along? Dad did.)

Work? School? Fun?
What are you talking about Dad?

It's time to start working on YOUR PLAN. Didn't I just say we were going to start working on YOUR PLAN at the end of the last chapter?

To get started on YOUR PLAN, we are headed back to English class.

… I've got a bad feeling about this.

Trust me, this is going to be good. I hope.

Section Simple

I call this first section, Section Simple.

This is where we are going to start figuring out the details of your vacation. Don't worry, it's going to be Simple (and Fun, and maybe even a little Magic). Trust me.

The 5 W's

One of the big lessons I learned in English class, back at ole Harrah High, was the use of the 5 W's.

You know, who, what, when, where, and why. Of course then they came along and added how, which kind of blew the whole W thing. I digress.

Those 5 W's and an H from English class will provide you with everything you really need to know in order to build YOUR PLAN.

Here is what we're going to cover in Section Simple:

- Why are you going to Walt Disney World?
- Who's going with you?
- When is the best time for you to go?
- Where are you going to eat?
- Where are you going to stay?
- What are you going to do while there?
- How are you going to get there?
- Plus, we'll make some reservations.

In each chapter, you'll find a Worksheet that will help you create YOUR PLAN. Be sure to download the Worksheets, fill them out and add them to your "trip bible."

Each Worksheet has some Simple, Fun, Magic questions that we will use for the Final Exam to help you build YOUR PLAN.

Dad's Bottom Line

Section Simple is where preparation for the BEST. VACATION. EVER. truly begins.

S

The Next Step

We are going to start by figuring out **Why** you are going to Walt Disney World. It might not be as obvious as you think.

School, 5W's, Worksheets, Final Exam…
I've got a bad feeling about this.

Trust me, this is going to be good.

You said that already, Dad.

Yes, I did, Pigment. Yes, I did.

NO, IT'S NOT OBVIOUS
WHY ARE YOU GOING TO WALT DISNEY WORLD?

"I'll be your skipper, guide, social director, and dance instructor
for the next three months."
- The Jungle Cruise*

The first thing you need to know before you start planning a Walt Disney World vacation. Do you know what it is?

Could it be who's going with us?

No, Pigment. That's important, but that's not the first thing.

How about when we are going?

That's another really important question, but it's not the first thing.

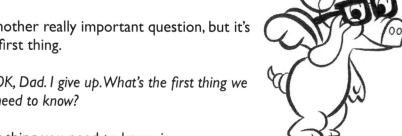

OK, Dad. I give up. What's the first thing we need to know?

The first thing you need to know is…

**The Jungle Cruise is a scenic boat ride featuring audio-animatronic animals and a live, comedic skipper in Adventureland at Magic Kingdom.*

Why are you going to Walt Disney World?

The dreaded "Why" question. Don't you just love it?

OK, it's been a long time since I had little kids running around, but let's see if I can nail this:

"Daddy, why does the sun go down? Daddy, why are you my Daddy? Daddy,, why can't I have cookies for dinner? Daddy, why do I have to go to bed now? Daddy, why don't we live at Disney World?"

Why is important to us. We always want to know "Why." Look at the news. What's important to us is not so much what happened, but Why it happened.

I think that knowing Why you are going to Walt Disney World is important. In fact, I think it's crucial.

The great philosopher, Yogi Berra once said:

> *"You've got to be very careful if you don't know where you are going, because you might not get there."*

Exactly right ,Yogi. That's what we are talking about here. Knowing Why we are going.

> *But Dad, Yogi said "Where," not "Why."*

Why yes, yes he did. And like Yogi, Dad's going to butcher the English language (and his quote) a bit. Try this: "You have to know Why you are going or you won't know if you had Fun." That's a Dad original.

> *Yogi you're not, Dad.*

That hurts Pigment. That really hurts.

Why is the most important question you can answer especially as we start to develop YOUR PLAN. Why are you going to Walt Disney World? No, it's not obvious.

Let me repeat that. **The most important question is: "Why are you going to Walt Disney World?"**

This is where some Magic comes into the process of making YOUR PLAN. Knowing Why you are going will give the trip a purpose. It gives it depth. It's no longer an ordinary vacation. It becomes… specialer (a great Yogi-like word).

Are you struggling with this? It's OK, Dad's got some ideas to help.

Some "Whys for taking a WDW Vacation"

- Rest and relaxation (if that's the case, you might want to think about changing your destination or going on a Disney Cruise)
- Spread your love of Disney to the kids
- See all of the new stuff at WDW
- Impart the love of Disney to a "Grumpy Gus"
- You want to go "Home"
- Little Janie wants to see Elsa and Anna
- Little Johnny wants to be a Jedi
- Everyone else does it
- You're "supposed" to take your kids to Disney
- Your sister is making you go

So what did you come up with? No, don't tell me… Write it down. Check out my handy, dandy Why Worksheet:

SimpleFunMagic.com/The-Why-Worksheet

The Theme

Now that you know the "Why," you can use it to give your trip a theme. Everything is better with a theme.

Have you ever heard a baseball team advertise like this: "It's regular old baseball night at the ballpark tonight. Come on out and join the Fun!" Nope, didn't think so.

Here's what you'll hear instead "Come on out to the ballpark on Monday for DOLLAR HOT DOG night. Enjoy some of our delicious ballpark hot dogs and root for the home team as they play their bitter division rivals in a critical mid-season game! No matter who wins, dollar hot dogs are always a home run!" A commercial writer I'm not, but you get the idea.

It's the theme that makes you want to go. A reason to come to the ballpark. A Why!

Your trip needs a Why.

We have started doing this for every trip.

In 2012, Mrs. Mom and I went on our first trip without kids in a long, long time.

When we were writing THE PLAN, we noticed we were doing a lot of things for the first time. So that became our theme. It became our Why. We even gave the trip a name – we called it our "New and Different" trip.

That's Why we were going to WDW - to try New and Different things. So, as much as possible, we did new things. We stayed in new hotels. We ate at new restaurants. We experienced attractions that we'd never ridden before. We even went on a Disney Cruise. Lots of New and Different. It was great.

I was talking to one of our staff members, who just got back from Walt Disney World. She said that all her kids wanted to do was to see the characters. So that's what they did. They arranged their whole PLAN around seeing the characters. Their trip was full of meet-and-greets, character meals, and making sure they filled up their autograph books. They called it their "Character Crawl" trip.

You need to know things like that when you create YOUR PLAN, because then you can structure YOUR PLAN around the things you want to experience.

So what's your answer? What's the theme of your trip or the most important thing you want to get out of it? What are you going to call YOUR trip?

Go over and download the Worksheet, fill it out and add it to your "trip bible."

Oh, and for some Fun, come over and tell me your Why and your trip name. I can't wait to hear what you've come up with.

Dad's Bottom Line

While this sounds a little silly, it's crucial for your Walt Disney World Vacation. When you know Why you are going, you can structure your plan to make sure you see what you want to see.

It's really that Simple, but it's a very powerful Magic trick. It will be Fun. I promise.

The Next Step

Next up, we take a look at Who is going. Maybe "Me and You and a Dog Named Boo?"

I like that song Dad.

Me too, Pigment. Me too.

ME AND YOU AND A...
WHO IS GOING WITH YOU?

"Imagination, imagination. A dream, can be a dream come true.
With just that spark, from me and you."
- Journey into Imagination with Figment*

Who is going with you? Who is going with you on the vacation of a lifetime? Who is... **GOING TO WALT DISNEY WORLD?!?!?!**

That's the question of the hour.

Oh, I know. It's going to be...

Am I right?

> Come on Dad. A dog named Boo? Who has a dog named Boo these days?

> I will say, that's the Simplest question you've asked so far. Most people are going to say, it'll be just me and the family.

*Journey Into Imagination with Figment is a dark ride attraction about the power of the five senses, located in the Imagination Pavilion at Epcot's Future World.

That's all. Drop the mic. Next...

In the immortal words of Lee Corso... not so fast my friend.

Who's Lee Corso?

You need to watch more college football Pigment.

I'll pass...

Yes, typically we just go with our immediate families, but you might want to think about some options. Let me help...

A love story

A girl and a boy are in love, but something happens and they break up. A couple of weeks later the girl wins a trip to Walt Disney World. On the trip a new guy chases her around WDW. She and the new guy ride Dumbo together, eat dinner at the Coral Reef Restaurant with the fishies swimming in the background. It's so romantic.

Unknown to the girl, the boy and his buddy have followed her to Disney World. They spend a whole day looking for her and finally spot her and see her with the new fella. It's really sad.

Finally the boy confronts the girl and it doesn't go well. He goes away. A little while later he finds the girl again and pours out his soul. She kisses him in front of the fountain in Epcot and the world is a happy place again.

Sound familiar? Maybe this will help:

SimpleFunMagic.com/The-Kiss

Who doesn't remember Cory and Topanga at Walt Disney World?* It was so sweet, so Magic. (They just don't make television like that these days.)

*Cory and Topanga were two of the central characters on Boy Meets World, a family sitcom that ran on ABC from 1993-2000.

Back in the 90s all the ABC sitcoms went to Walt Disney World and all of those shows had one thing in common.

What was that "one thing" Dad?

The extras

All of those 90s sitcoms that went to Walt Disney World had one thing in common. There were always "extras" on the trip. Not just the family. Not film extras, but extra people from the shows.

Full House had Kimmie and Steve. On *Family Matters* the Winslow's tagged along with Urkel. For *Sabrina the Teenage Witch* there was a class trip and *Rosanne* took the whole family, including the boyfriend.

Yes, the *Boy Meets World* episode didn't have the whole family, but even that one makes the point.

What point would that be?

A Walt Disney World vacation is all about Who is going. It really makes all the difference in your enjoyment of the trip.

Yes, most of the time Who's going is Simple. But, sometimes, it's a whole lot of Fun to expand your horizons and think outside the box. It can be Magic to add a few extras.

Magic? You sure? Let me ask, who are these "extras" you propose we take along?

The extended family

One of our best trips ever was when we took the whole family. Our family, Mrs. Mom's Mom and Dad, Mrs. Mom's sisters and their kids. 15 in all. It was an incredible experience. We still talk about it whenever we get together. We made a lot of priceless memories.

Memories like the time we all ate dinner at 'Ohana. We'd been there a while and a big group came and sat at the table next to us. They saw we were having a great time and asked the waiter for the same thing we were drinking. They couldn't believe it when the waiter told them Coke and iced tea.

Oh, and the night that the baby of the bunch (he was 4) ran down the hall of the Polynesian Resort buck naked because it was his night to sleep in Grandma and Grandpa's room. He was in a big hurry.

Those memories are etched on our minds. That's what it's all about. Walt Disney World was built for families. That was Walt's dream.

> *Uh, Dad. Do you really want me to take my whole family? Do you know how many people that would be? I have like 30 brothers and sisters. Not a chance. There's no way. That would be a nightmare.*

Oh, come on Pigment. It would be Fun. It would be like...

Or maybe not... but it's something to think about.

Other extras

Typically, we think of family first when it comes to going to WDW with extras, but there are many other options.

I know a lot of people who go with friends, neighbors, people from church, work, convention buddies, and random people off the street.

> *Really Dad? Random people off the street?*

Sure. It would be just like *Finding Nemo!* That whole movie was about shared experiences with random people.

So, did that spark anything? Are you thinking about Who you would go to Walt Disney World with?

Who do you want smiling along with you in all of the Memory Maker* pictures?

It's time to write it down. Yes, write it down. (Hey, if you don't write it down it didn't happen, right?)

⬇ SimpleFunMagic.com/The-Who-Worksheet

Take a minute to download the Worksheet, fill it out and put it in your "trip bible."

Dad! Dad! Dad!

Yes Pigment. I see your "hand" is up. Do you have a question?

Yes, since we're talking about who is going, and making memories, writing things down and all that, can I ask a quick question?

I think you just did, but go on.

Funny guy. Say I have a two-year-old… should I take him or her to Walt Disney World?

That's really a great question, Pigment.

OK, are you going to answer it?

I'm thinking about it.

But you are writing. Can't you just "think about it" on your own time and write your answer so we don't have to sit here and wait for it?

Yes, I could do that, but it wouldn't be as dramatic (or annoying, take your pick).

Getting paid by the word again are we?

*Memory Maker part of My Disney Experience. It's a program where you can download and purchase pictures taken by Disney PhotoPass photographers and pictures taken automatically on some attractions.

I represent that remark. (*Ha Ha, Dad.*)

Let's see… Two-year-olds at Walt Disney World…

The perfect age for a first trip to Walt Disney World?

Pigment, I think a better way to phrase that question is, "what is the perfect age to go to Walt Disney World for the first time?"

I used to be in the "perfect age is five-years-old club." Not anymore.

Walt Disney World is for everyone. (And no this is not just me spouting the Disney company line. I have no affiliation with Disney other than that I'm a big fan.) I really believe that WDW is for everyone. Even two-year-olds.

Let me explain.

I keep saying this, but it's so true. Walt Disney World is a place to create memories. Memories that you will talk about for the rest of your life.

> *But Dad, a two year old isn't going to remember anything.*

That's true, but their parents will.

It's not about creating memories for the two-year-old; it's about creating memories for the two-year-old's parents, grandparents, brothers, sisters, aunts, uncles, and friends.

There is nothing more precious than seeing the reaction a little one has when they meet Mickey for the first time. When they take their first ride on Dumbo. Even when they fall asleep in The Enchanted Tiki Room* (yes, I'm talking about you, Man-Child).

Those are memories that you just can't get anywhere else. YOUR MEMORIES!

The Enchanted Tiki Room is a musical show performed by audio-animatronic birds in Adventureland in Magic Kingdom.

OK Dad, one more question. what about, how do I say this nicely, the more "experienced" family members? Like the Grandparents?

Experienced? Nice word. I'm glad you said it and I didn't.
I'll make this short.

First time for everything.

Ouch. That hurts.

I'll say it again, Walt's dream was to build a theme park that was for EVERYONE! From the baby (yes, I've even heard of six-day-old babies going to WDW) all the way up to great, great grandma and grandpa.

Walt Disney World is for EVERYONE!!! Everyone who can create a memory for themselves and for others.

Dad's Bottom Line

The bottom line is Who do you want to experience Walt Disney World with? Who will you want to share lifetime memories with and about?

That's where you start.

Typically, it will be the immediate family, but think about branching out from there.

This isn't hard. In fact, it's pretty Simple, but the results can be Magic. Think about Who can you go to WDW with to have the most Fun.

Don't forget to fill out the Worksheet.

SimpleFunMagic.com/The-Who-Worksheet

Fill it out and add it to your "trip bible."

OK, so now we know Who is going to share our vacation of a lifetime. It's time to come on over and tell dear ole Dad Who's going along with you.

SimpleFunMagic.com/Share-The-Who

Now wasn't that Fun?

The Next Step

Now we're going to figure out When to go
to WDW. Yes, another Simple question with
a Magical answer.

> *Can we go to Walt Disney World
> now Dad?*

No, Pigment. Not now.

3

EASY OR HARD
WHEN ARE YOU GOING TO GO?

"Howdy folks. If you're just joining us, welcome aboard!"
- The Walt Disney World Railroad*

One of the questions I'm asked the most is, "When should I go to Walt Disney World?"

It's a question that's either easy or hard to answer.

> *"Easy or hard?" Hey Dad, you're not making any sense.*
> *Again.*

Look, Pigment. I typed very plainly and I meant exactly what I said. Choosing When to go to Walt Disney World is either easy or hard. That makes it an easy or a hard question.

> *"Lucy, I think you got some splainin' to do."*

You're so Funny. Listen...

*The Walt Disney Railroad is an attraction/transportation method that circles Magic Kingdom park with stops at Main Street U.S.A., Frontierland, Storybook Circus, and Tomorrowland.

Choosing When to go to Walt Disney World might be as easy as when Daddy or Mommy can get off work, that's when we go. It can be as hard as trying to coordinate the schedules of the whole gang.

I have written a whole lot about the Best Time to Visit Walt Disney World. It's kind of Dad's signature thing.

So, you are probably wondering when is the Best Time to Visit Walt Disney World? Come on, admit it. You were.

Ok, Dad. I admit, it did flash through my mind.

It's a mind control thing. I'm pretty good at it.

Dad, don't hurt your arm patting yourself on the back. When is the Best Time to Visit Walt Disney World?

The Best Time to Visit Walt Disney World is…

This is profound.

You've got to see this.

Are you ready?

You sure?

The Best Time to Visit Walt Disney World is…

Anytime You Can.

Simple as that.

I read through all of that for "anytime you can"? Can you be just a bit LESS helpful?

(Chuckle) I doubt it.

At least it was Fun for one of us.

Dad do you know what sound a one handed clap makes?

OK, I'll be serious. (Maybe.)

I mean it. The Best Time for a trip of a lifetime to Walt Disney World is whenever you can arrange it. It is always a good time to go to Walt Disney World. By the way, what's the ONE BIG THING?

Remember?

It's really that Simple. Going to Disney World is Fun! And it's always Magic!

Sometimes, When you can go to Walt Disney World might be out of your hands. Work, school, and family committments can limit your choices for When to go.

That's OK. If that's when you can go, that's when you can go. But if you have some options, choosing When to go to WDW gets hard.

Yes, Dad can help.

But first, go over to the website and download the When Worksheet and fill out the Simple section.

SimpleFunMagic.com/The-When-Worksheet

Next let's look at…

The best time to visit Walt Disney World

There are four factors to consider when looking for the Best Time to Visit WDW. Those factors are…

• **Crowds** – This is the biggie. Crowds can vary from nice and calm to CrAzy and OuT of coNTrOL. On Christmas Day the Magic Kingdom will close to new guests around 11:00 AM. The Magic Kingdom holds somewhere around 140,000 guests. That's CrAzy and OuT of coNTrOL. Completely and totally.

On a slow day in September you'll be hard pressed to find 15,000 people in the Magic Kingdom. That's a big, big difference.

• **Prices** – This one is pretty Simple. Prices, for the most part, follow crowds. The higher the crowds, the higher the prices. The lower the crowds, the lower the prices and the bigger the discounts.

• **Weather** – Some people (like Dad) think about the weather before we choose when to go to WDW. I've been to WDW in late July and early August, when the heat index hovers just below the boiling point of water. Been there, done that, not ever going back (famous last words).

If you are bothered by heat, you might want to consider some of the cooler months of the year (November - February).

• **Events** – One thing that separates Disney from other theme parks is their events. A whole lot of people PLAN vacations based on the events at WDW.

Marathons, festivals, parties, concert series, and holiday celebrations draw people to WDW. Going during the events is one of the BEST reasons to visit Walt Disney World. Especially during the Christmas season. (Dad loves Christmas at WDW.)

Be sure to keep in mind one, or all, of these as you choose When to go to WDW.

MONTH-BY-MONTH AT WDW

	CROWDS	PRICES	WEATHER	EVENTS
JAN	▮	$	☀ COOL	🎨 👟
FEB	▆	$$	☀ COOL	🎨 👟
MAR	▇	$$$$$	☀ WARM	🌷
APR	▅	$$$$	☀ WARM	🌷 👟
MAY	▃	$$$	☀ WARM	🌷
JUN	▃	$$$$	🌧 HOT	
JUL	▅	$$$$$	🌧 HOT	🎆
AUG	▃	$$$	⛈ HOT	🍽 🎃
SEP	▮	$	⛈ HOT	🍽 🎃
OCT	▅	$$	☀ WARM	🍽 🎃
NOV	▆	$$$	☀ COOL	🍽 🎄 👟
DEC	▇	$$$$$	☀ COOL	🎄

WDW EVENT LEGEND

EPCOT INTERNATIONAL FESTIVAL OF THE ARTS

EPCOT INTERNATIONAL FOOD & WINE FESTIVAL

EPCOT INTERNATIONAL FLOWER & GARDEN FESTIVAL

RUNDISNEY EVENTS

FOURTH OF JULY

MICKEY'S NOT SO SCARY HALLOWEEN PARTY

MICKEY'S VERY MERRY CHRISTMAS PARTY

Isn't that chart cool?

So, what does your month look like? Is it a good month to go?

Grab your Worksheet and fill in the details in the Fun section.

SimpleFunMagic.com/The-When-Worksheet

You might want to check out the details of When you are thinking about going. For more details about crowds, weather, prices and events, I've created a special page over on the website you might want to check out.

SimpleFunMagic.com/The-Best-Time

There is enough there to help you choose your perfect time to visit. Remember, this is YOUR vacation – think about what matters most to YOU and those traveling with YOU.

Now that you've got an idea and you've filled out the Worksheet, come share When are you going to Walt Disney World. Who knows, maybe I'll be there at the same time and I can meet you. I'd really like that.

SimpleFunMagic.com/Share-The-When

Now that we know Who, What and Why, let's have a little Fun.

Let's make a Rough Draft of our trip.

The Rough Draft

Now it's time to sketch out a rough day-to-day plan or a Rough Draft of what you are going to do each day of your trip. At this point we just want a general idea.

We'll do a lot more work on this later, but as we get started (and especially for the next chapter) it's important to think about where we want to be each day.

Day 0, Day 1, Day 2...

The first step in creating YOUR Rough Draft is to make a general plan of what you are going to do each day of your trip. No, not minute by minute, but just a Rough Draft. Day 0 – Travel Day, Day 1 - Magic Kingdom, Day 2 – Epcot, etc.

> *But Dad, don't we need to know crowd levels, weather, which park is the best on which day, and all that?*

We'll come back to that in a little while, Pigment. But for now, let's keep it Simple.

Arrival Day

The perfect Rough Draft starts with the Arrival Day, or as I call it, Day 0.

Day 0 can be tricky depending on your arrival time.

If you are flying, and land in the afternoon, should you PLAN time in the parks? What happens if flights are delayed? What if the car breaks down? What time do the parks close? What if grandma gets run over by a reindeer? (Just checking to make sure you're still reading.)

We experienced some trouble on Day 0 when we went with the whole gang to Mickey's Very Merry Christmas Party. Check out what can happen on Day 0:

Mickey's Very Merry Christmas Party is a hard ticket, after hours, special event held select nights at Magic Kingdom in November and December.

When we took the whole gang, we arrived on the very last Mickey's Very Merry Christmas Party* date. Most of us wanted to go to the party, so we bought tickets.

We weren't all traveling together. We came in two groups. The first group was scheduled to arrive at the Orlando Airport at 2 pm, and the second, at 5 pm. We were in the first group and had no problems getting to the Magic Kingdom right when we could first get in using our party tickets (4 pm).

The second group wasn't so lucky.

Their flight was delayed. The first delay wasn't too bad, but then there were a couple more delays and they ended up getting to the Magic Kingdom right around 8:30 pm. They met us just in time for the parade and the fireworks.

For them going to the Party probably wasn't the best idea.

Day 0 can be tricky to PLAN. A pretty good rule of thumb is if you are arriving before 3 pm you can enjoy some time in the parks. Epcot is almost always open until 9 pm or later and on busy days the other parks will stay open late too.

If you arrive early there are always some Fun ways to make a great first impression and there are a lot of restaurants you can walk in to without reservations.

SimpleFunMagic.com/Arrival-Day-Ideas

Danger Will Robinson:
Making Advanced Dining Reservations (ADRs) for Day 0 is not a good idea. If you miss your reservation, Disney will charge you $10 per person. I hate it when that happens.

As you get an arrival day idea, go over and write it down on the Rough Draft Worksheet.

SimpleFunMagic.com/The-Rough-Draft-Worksheet

Day 1

Which Park do you go to on your first day, Day 1? I could say, "This is the most important day of the whole trip. This is When the trip of a lifetime starts and the tone is set." But that's not really true.

Every day is important. Memories will be made every day of the trip so, don't obsess over Day 1.

When the kids were little, we'd employ the strategy of doing Epcot first. It was a "get it out of the way" type of thing.

These days, we pretty much start with the Magic Kingdom. We LOVE the Magic Kingdom, so we try to begin and end each trip in there if possible. (But if the schedule doesn't work we'll start wherever.) Look, there is no wrong answer here.

So you've written down Day 1 on your Rough Draft Worksheet. Now do the same thing for Day 2, Day 3, and so on for your whole trip. Again, don't stress. It's a Rough Draft. It might change later.

I told you this was going to be Simple.

We'll come back and beef up some details later, but now you have a Rough Draft of your trip. Aren't you proud? Isn't this Fun?!

Let's Celebrate!!!!!!!

SimpleFunMagic.com/Rough-Draft-Celebration

Dad's Bottom Line

There are only 365 choices (366 in leap years) for the best day to visit Walt Disney World, and every one of them makes sense for someone (or a lot of someones).

Choosing your dates for your trip of a lifetime may be easy, or it may be hard, but either way, remember, the One Big Thing...

YOU'RE GOING TO WALT DISNEY WORLD!

Now that's Fun.

The Next Step

Next, we need to have to talk about what there is to do at Walt Disney World. It's not much.

> *Not much to do? Are you crazy?*
> *There's so much to do at WDW I don't*
> *know if I'll ever be able to do it all.*

That just might be true, Pigment. It might be true.

SO MUCH TO DO
WHAT WILL YOU DO WHEN YOU GET THERE?

"I'm walking right down the middle of Main Street U.S.A.
It's the heart of America, the heartbeat of a holiday.
The place was made with a Magical plan
And just around the corner is a Fantasyland."
- The Dapper Dans*

Time for a status check. So far, we've talked about the Why, the Who (no, not the rock band), and the When. Now it's time to take a look at What are you going to do when you get to the Most Magical Place on Earth.

What to do?

Walt Disney World is HUGE and there's a whole lot to do! In fact, there is more to do at Walt Disney World than you could do if you stayed a whole week or even two. I know, I've tried.

*Come on Dad, you're exaggerating.
There can't be that much to do!
A whole week? TWO?! There's no way.*

*The Dapper Dans are a barbershop quartet who perform on Main Street U.S.A. in Magic Kingdom.

Yes, a whole week and even two. One week at WDW is enough to get a good start, but you won't see everything. And if you want to see some other things around Orlando…

Forty square miles

Walt Disney World is forty square miles in area. That's more than double the size of Manhattan (no, not Manhattan, Kansas… Manhattan as in New York City). Let's put it another way – it's the size of San Francisco.

Over 62,000 people WORK at Walt Disney World. It's the biggest single site employer in the United States. On an average day, there are over 150,000 visitors at Walt Disney World.

At Walt Disney World there are…

Walt Disney World has four theme parks. In those parks are over seventy attractions and shows plus hundreds of restaurants and gift shops. It takes a full day or more to see everything in each park.

Depending on how you count, there are twenty-eight* Disney owned Resorts and more being built all the time. Those Resorts have over 27,000 rooms.

The Resorts are destinations in themselves. One of my favorite things to do is to go and look at each of the Resorts, especially at Christmas time, when all the special decorations are up.

In addition to the Disney Resorts, there are fourteen non-Disney owned hotels and resorts on the property. These include a Holiday Inn, several independently owned hotels, and even a Waldorf Astoria.

We are just getting started. There are:

- 2 huge water parks
- An entertainment complex with over 150 shops and restaurants
- Over 100 resort shops, restaurants, and entertainment options
- 4 mini-golf courses

*There are co-located Resorts in some locations. For example, the Contemporary Resort and Bay Lake Tower Resort are in the same location and share amenities but are "officially" two different Resorts.

- 3 full golf courses plus a 9-hole junior course
- A sports complex, a nightlife area
- 3 spas
- 14.7 miles of Monorail track
- Over 160 miles of roads
- Marinas with water sports
- More than 750 water craft (the world's largest private navy), which travel hundreds of miles of waterways around the complex.

I've been to Walt Disney World over 20 times, and there are still parts of it I've never seen.

And that's just inside the gates of Walt Disney World.

Outside the "World"

Within a 90-minute drive from Walt Disney World you've got:

- Universal Studios Orlando (2 theme parks and a water park)
- SeaWorld Orlando (1 theme park and 2 water parks)
- LEGOLAND Florida
- Busch Gardens in Tampa Bay
- Kennedy Space Center
- Two cruise ship terminals (one is home to the Disney Cruise Line),
- Several outlet malls and luxury shopping centers
- Hundreds of miles of beaches
- One of the premier NASCAR racetracks
- Golf courses galore
- Loads of small attractions, shops, restaurants and other things

Plus, Major League Baseball, NFL Football, NBA Basketball, NHL Hockey, MLS Soccer are all in either Orlando or Tampa Bay.

You could literally spend twelve hours a day, every day for months trying to see all there is to see in and around Walt Disney World and you would still not see everything.

Uh Dad. I'm a bit overwhelmed. Twelve hours a day for months? I can't do that. I only have a few days for my vacation. But there's so much to do. How am I going to do it all?

That's the point, Pigment. You can't do it all so we have to figure out What you are going to do while you are there. It all starts with…

How many days

There is one Simple question that will be the basis for figuring out What you are going to do at WDW: **How many days can you afford to be at Walt Disney World?**

I told you it was a Simple question.

What do you mean by how long can I "afford" to be at WDW?

I mean exactly that. How long can you afford to be there? How long can you take off work? Is your trip during school holidays and you have to get back? How much can you spend (remember, you have a budget!) and how many days will that buy?

OK, I get it, but what if it's not very much. Like 3 days?

That's OK. While there is a lot to do at Walt Disney World, you don't have to do it all every time you go.

But how am I going to figure out what I want to do during my 3 days?

We'll get to that in just a minute, but first you need to write down How long you can afford to be at WDW on the What Worksheet.

Hop over to the website and download it. The first section is for how long you can afford to be at WDW. Just check one of the boxes.

SimpleFunMagic.com/The-What-Worksheet

What would YOU like to do

Since this is YOUR vacation, we probably want to see what YOU would like to do. Right?

OK, that's the Fun part of the What Worksheet. What do you like to do on vacation? Me, I like to go to WDW and spend all day in the parks running (OK, maybe walking very slowly) from ride to ride. I'm a ride junkie. YOU on the other hand might be a pool person, or a foodie that just wants to eat around the world.

The important thing is that this is YOUR vacation, so what do you want to do on your trip?

Pull out the Worksheet again and fill out the Fun section.

SimpleFunMagic.com/The-What-Worksheet

What to Do Tool

Would you like to see a little Magic?

Magic, I love Magic!

This is amazing. Over on the website we've created a Simple little tool that will take your What answers and tell you What to do on YOUR vacation.

Dad, I hate to interrupt…

Then why do you keep doing it?

Because it's why you created me.

Good point.

If this tool thingy you created tells me What I should do then how is it MY trip, not YOUR trip? Aren't you being a little bit of a hypocrite saying "don't listen to anyone else" and "you are going to plan YOUR vacation" but then your little tool tell us what to do?

You might look at it that way, but I think if you try the tool out, you'll see that it gives you some options and tries to find what is best for you based on your likes and desires.

OK...? I guess.

Tell you what, go over to the website and give it a try. Or as the old saying goes... "Try it, you'll like it."

Um, Dad. If I remember right that saying ended, "So I tried it. Thought I was going to die."

Oh, I think you're right Pigment. Maybe that wasn't the best choice of sayings (chuckle).

I promise you won't die, you might even have a little Fun.

Using the tool, together, we'll take a tour of all there is to do at Walt Disney World and outside the "World." It will be Fun. Trust me. We've made it Simple, and Tink* herself has flown over and doused it with Magic.

You probably know what time it is. It's time to fill out the Magic section of your What Worksheet. Go ahead...

Now wasn't all of that Simple? Wasn't it Fun? Isn't that tool Magic?

Save that Worksheet in your "Trip bible." We'll come back to it later.

Oh, and while you're at it, why don't you pop over to the website and share What you'll be doing at WDW?

*Tink is short for Tinker Bell, Peter Pan's pixie sidekick in the 1953 Disney Animated Classic, Peter Pan. She' even has her own series of direct-to-video movies with DisneyToon Studios.

Dad's Bottom Line

There really is a lot to do on a Disney World vacation. An awful lot. The Magic Kingdom itself takes about 2 days to tour. I had a Disney Travel Representative recently tell me the average stay at WDW is now 6 days.

You could literally spend weeks at Walt Disney World and not experience everything. It's that big.

Check out Dad's What To Do Tool and YOU will get a good idea about What YOU should plan to do during YOUR stay.

The Next Step

Next, we need to figure out Where to eat.
(Don't anyone tell Pigment. He eats like a pig.)

Is someone talking about eating?
I like to eat.

Yes you do, Pigment. Yes you do.

5

LET'S EAT
WHERE ARE YOU GOING TO DINE AT WDW?

"One blustery day in the Hundred-Acre Wood,
a little bear named Winnie the Pooh set off in search of honey."
- The Many Adventures of Winnie the Pooh*

It's time for the best part of planning a Walt Disney World vacation. It's time to eat!

*Are you kidding Dad? Eat? At a time like this?
Of course I'm going to eat, I'm stressed. I've already
gone through a whole bag of chips. Now you're
telling me I need to eat more?
What's going on?*

Time to eat

Yes, it's time to Eat! You need to get started on this TODAY! Trust me!

*OK, I'm headed to the pantry. What now?
Should I break out the emergency Snickers?*

*The Many Adventures of Winnie the Pooh is a dark ride in Fantasyland at the Magic Kingdom which is based on the classic A.A. Milne stories about Christopher Robin and his friends in the Hundred Acre Wood.

No, silly. I'm not talking about actually eating right now.

THEN WHAT ON EARTH ARE YOU TALKING ABOUT?

Easy there, Pigment. Down boy! Let me explain. I'm talking about working on Where you are going to eat on a Walt Disney World vacation.

> *But Dad, that's months away. Do we have to talk about that right now? What am I supposed to do with this Snickers?*

Oh, I can't resist...

That was way too easy...

OK, I've got to get serious. This really is important. But now I've got that silly song running through my head. Eat it, eat it...

Follow your eating patterns from home

Before we dive in to the restaurants, I have one big piece of advice. You might want to take into consideration your typical eating patterns at home before you look at the menus – it's really easy for your eyes to be bigger than your stomach at Walt Disney World!

If you eat a light breakfast, an energy bar for lunch and a healthy dinner all the time at home but expect to eat three big, juicy, carb packed meals a day just because you are on vacation, you are going to have problems.

Don't change your whole lifestyle just because you are on vacation. Yes, if you don't exercise a lot at home, there will be more physical activity and you might need a little more protein than you usually consume, but don't go all crazy.

Think about your eating patterns at home. Fill that out in the Simple section of the Worksheet.

But Dad, but Dad, we're on vacation. Can't we splurge a little?

Good point Pigment.

Vacation equals splurging

Every time Mrs. Mom and I plan a trip we start by looking at things like the kind of dishes we've seen on the Food Network on TV. I know. Sounds silly, but Dad and Mrs. Mom are wannabe foodies.

That goes for our trips to Walt Disney World too. We almost always splurge on at least one meal that doesn't follow our eating patterns at home.

There's nothing wrong with that. Vacation does equal splurging. Hey, it's a vacation and there should be a Dole Whip*, some good food, and maybe even a Premium Mickey Bar** or three.

But, just don't overdo it. You'll thank me.

Choosing restaurants can be Fun

The first thing you need to do is to decide Where you want to make reservations. This is not as easy as it sounds. There are literally hundreds of dining options at Walt Disney World. Narrowing them down can be difficult.

Mrs. Mom and I usually spend several of our walks deciding Where to eat. It's one of the highlights of our day. If we have a trip upcoming (and we usually do) we'll talk about the PLAN.

The first few weeks when we discuss the PLAN, we talk about Where to eat. We always start out talking about the Table Service restaurants we want to visit.

Mrs. Mom starts a list of the ones that sound interesting. Yes, she writes them down and puts them in her "trip bible." You should too.

So let's do just that.

---

*Dole whip is a pineapple soft serve available at select locations at WDW that has a cult following. **Premium Mickey Bars are Mickey-shaped, chocolate coated vanilla ice cream novelties widely available at the WDW parks and resorts.*

SimpleFunMagic.com/The-Where-To-Eat-Worksheet

Ummmm, Dad. How are they supposed to know which restaurants they want to try? Hmmmm?

Nice job teeing up the next section Pigment. Thanks.

That's my job.

There are hundreds of choices of Where to eat at WDW (yes, I've already said that, but it's important enough to say again). So, I've created a "Where To Eat Tool" that will make suggestions for restaurants to fit your preferences.

You've got to see this:

SimpleFunMagic.com/Where-To-Eat-Tool

Oh, while we're talking about choosing restaurants, don't forget…

Eating is not a Solo Sport

Dad, I think you have a typo there.
Shouldn't that be PLANNING, not Eating Is Not A Solo Sport?

Nope. I said Eating, I meant Eating!

Are you going to explain?

If I must…

If it's not too much trouble.

OK, here goes, back in the "If You Don't Have A PLAN" chapter, I talked about how PLANNING is not a Solo Sport. The same is true for choosing Where to eat. YOU (unless you are going alone) are not going to eat alone. Profound, right?

That means that you need to check with your travel partners to see Where everyone wants to eat. Yes, everyone.

Now before Pigment jumps in here and says something pithy about needing help let me say, I've got a very helpful spreadsheet that will help you figure out Where everyone wants to eat.

Check this out…

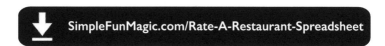

SimpleFunMagic.com/Rate-A-Restaurant-Spreadsheet

It's really Simple and Fun to fill out. Everyone rates each restaurant (the research is the best part) and the restaurant with the most points should be on the top of the list. Magic!

Eating at WDW is part of the experience

One of my favorite places to eat at Walt Disney World is Casey's Corner in the Magic Kingdom. Casey's is a hot dog joint that sells hot dogs and French Fries. No, the hot dogs are not anything special, but there's just something special about stopping at Casey's.

Stopping at Casey's is kind of like having a hot dog at a ballgame. It's part of the experience. Casey's is even themed after a ballgame. It gets its theme from Casey at the Bat.* There is all kinds of baseball memorabilia on the walls.

Eating at Walt Disney World is a big part of your trip. The restaurants at WDW all have themes and are part of the "show." A big part of your trip of a lifetime is experiencing "dining at WDW."

Another one of my favorite dining experiences at Walt Disney World is the Sci-Fi Dine-In Theater Restaurant. It is so cool!!!

How cool is it Dad?

The temperature is usually about 68 degrees but that's not what's so cool about it (I couldn't resist).

Casey at the Bat is a baseball poem written in 1888 Ernest Thayer, which was adapted into an animated short for the Disney film Make Mine Music in 1946.

The Sci-Fi Dine-In is a restaurant that's set up like a Drive-In Movie Theater. You sit in "cars" and watch the big movie screen, all in a soundstage decked out to look like you're under the night sky. They show trailers for old black and white monster movies. It's so corny.

It's just something that has to be experienced.

From the Simple hot dog at Casey's Corner all the way up to the elegant Victoria and Albert's restaurant, all of the Walt Disney World restaurants are something you have to experience. They are amazing.

Why dining at Walt Disney World needs a PLAN

In addition to narrowing down your handful of meals and snacks from hundreds of options, there are some really unique elements of dining at WDW that we need to go over.

I'm only going to give you the Simple information here since not everyone needs all of the details, but there are links for more information if you need to find out more about how something applies to your trip of a lifetime.

> • **Types of Restaurants:** Disney has 3 main types of restaurants. Quick Service locations are casual eateries for snacks and meals where you place an order, pay, pick up your food and seat yourself. Table Service spots are "sit down" restaurants where a server takes your order and brings your food (although sometimes these are buffets) and some of these spots offer dining with characters. Signature restaurants are similar to Table Service but they offer more expensive menu items and usually have a dress code.

> Read about the different restaurants on Dad's Guide to WDW: dadsguidetowdw.com/disney-world-restaurants.html

> • **Advanced Dining Reservations:** Since so many guests visit WDW every day, there is a huge demand for many of the most popular restaurants. So just like in the "real" world, you can make reservations for all of the Table Service and Signature restaurants at WDW. Unlike the "real" world, you really do need to make reservations if you want a table – many book up 6 months in advance! That's right – you can make your Advanced Dining Reservations (or ADRs) 180 days before your trip.

Read all about making ADRs on Dad's Guide to WDW:
dadsguidetowdw.com/advanced-dining-reservations.html

• **The Disney Dining Plan:** In an effort to curb the sticker shock that can happen at WDW and make families feel a sense of ease on their Magical vacations, there is an optional Disney Dining Plan available to guests of Disney resort hotels. Basically, you pick from one of three packages which entitle you to a certain number of snacks and meals each day. It sure is convenient, but Dad's not a fan since it usually doesn't save you any money. It all depends on your eating habits.

Learn about the Disney Dining Plan and use
Dad's Disney Dining Plan Calculator on Dad's Guide to WDW:
dadsguidetowdw.com/disney-dining-plan.html

• **Discounts:** Select restaurants offer discounts to Annual Passholders, DVC Members, or Tables in Wonderland card holders. If you're a first time or infrequent visitor these probably don't apply to you, but if you plan to visit often they are worth looking into.

• **Allergies and Special Diets:** Disney does an outstanding job of catering to guests with allergies and special diets. At any restaurant (even Quick Service locations) you can see a list of all the ingredients in any dish, and many times there will be an option listed to accommodate allergies (for instance, swapping out a wheat bun for a gluten free bun, or leaving strawberries off your fruit plate).

At Table Service and Signature Restaurants, depending on the dishes offered on the regular menu the chef might make a special item just for you – even at buffets! All you need to do is alert the person taking your order and you'll be allowed to speak with a manager or chef to get your meal sorted.

Once you've got all your research gathered, share where you plan to eat! at WDW:

SimpleFunMagic.com/Share-Where-To-Eat

Dad's Bottom Line

Choosing Where to eat at Walt Disney World may be the "Funnest" part of the planning process. Just remember, Eating is not a Solo Sport.

Let everyone get involved in picking which restaurants you want to experience on your trip.

The Next Step

Nighty-night time. Yes, it's time to talk about Where to Sleep.

Oooh, Oooh. Sleeping is one of my favorite things to do. Which hotel has the best pigpen, Dad?

Pigpen? I don't think so, Pigment. I don't think so.

6

SLEEPY TIME
WHERE ARE YOU GOING TO SLEEP?

**"The next time you check into a deserted hotel on the
dark side of Hollywood, make sure you know
just what kind of vacancy you're filling."
– The Twilight Zone Tower of Terror***

Wow, I'm full. Wasn't that Fun?

So, now that we know Why we are going to WDW, Who is coming with us,
When we are visiting, and Where we are going to eat. It's time to look at
Where we are going to sleep.

Are you ready for this?

OK, buckle down. Here we go…

*But Dad, I thought you were going to make
this Fun. I don't like the sound of "buckle down."*

Have you ever been to a theme park? What happens
right before the Funnest rides start? They buckle you
in. Right? So buckle in, and let's have some Fun!

**The Twilight Zone Tower of Terror is a paranormal thrill ride at the end of Sunset Boulevard in
Disney's Hollywood Studios.*

Where are you going to sleep?

The old song Nashville Cats says…

♫ SimpleFunMagic.com/Nashville-Cats

What on earth does Nashville Cats *have to do with* Where we are going to sleep *when we go to Walt Disney World?*

Ah, that's a good question. Sit back and learn. This might be Fun!

When it comes to Where to sleep at Walt Disney World, there are about thirteen hundred and fifty-two options. I'm serious.

Thirteen hundred and fifty-two?

Yes, thirteen hundred and fifty-two. Check this out. The official Orlando visitor's site says there are over 400 hotels in Orlando alone.

Answers.com says the number is 800. If you do a search for hotels around Walt Disney World on Kayak.com it brings back 1,144 listings. Booking.com has 2410 in Orlando! That doesn't count all the rental houses, campgrounds, and whatever other options you might have.

Thirteen hundred and fifty-two isn't sounding so crazy now is it?

Oh, my goodness. Dad, you're not helping! Now I'm really stressed. What am I going to do? How am I going to choose? When is the Fun going to start?

Hey, this is Fun for one of us (evil laugh).

Let's start narrowing down those 1,352 options and find the one that's right for you. Maybe we can help Pigment be a little less stressed.

I like that idea.

Just a bed?

There are a couple of schools of thought when it comes to choosing Where to sleep. A lot of people say, "it's just a bed, get the cheapest one." The other camp says, "it's all part of the experience, get the most you can afford."

Of course, then there's the third option of, "I'm on vacation, I want to splurge and stay IN THE CASTLE!" (Don't go getting your hopes up – while there is a suite in Cinderella Castle, it's not for sale – you can only stay here by invitation.)

The first thing (in my opinion) that you need to look at when you are trying to decide Where to stay is, "what does your travel party think about hotels? Is it just a bed, or is it an experience?"

> *Worksheet time?*

Yes, it's Worksheet time.

SimpleFunMagic.com/The-Where-To-Sleep-Worksheet

The Simple section will help you figure out how you think about Where to sleep.

Onsite or offsite?

The next thing we need to decide when looking at Where to sleep on the trip of a lifetime is whether or not to sleep on Disney Property.

I'm going to say this upfront: I've tried both, and I vastly prefer sleeping in a Disney Hotel. But I'm kind of a Disney nut.

> *You can say that again.*

I'll try to be neutral here, but I warn you, it will be hard.

When it comes to whether to sleep offsite or on Disney property there are a series of things to consider.

Money, money, money, money

The number one thing to consider when you are trying to Plan Where to sleep is...

Oooh, Oooh, I know this one… Can I, can I?

Sure go ahead…

A twin spin. Thanks Pigment. I love those songs. No, not because of the topic, they just sound cool. OK, the topic is pretty cool too.

Yep, it all starts with money.

Let's face it. Disney hotels are expensive. There, I said it. It's true. You can save a lot of money by sleeping offsite (we'll talk about what you give up in a little bit).

A few months ago, I was talking to a guy who works at one of the companies that rents houses near Walt Disney World. These are nice houses. He said you could get a 5-bedroom house, with a kitchen and a private screened in pool for less than it costs to stay at a Disney Value Resort.

That's just crazy, and it wasn't an isolated example. I talked to a different company and it was the same story. You can definitely save a lot of money by renting a house offsite.

The same is true for hotels. Comparable class lodging outside of the Walt Disney World gates is cheaper than inside.

Lodging is not the only thing that you can save on by sleeping offsite. There is a wide variety of less expensive dining options when you sleep offsite. There are more entertainment options (as if you needed any more of those), and lots of other things offsite that you don't have onsite.

In the immortal words of Forrest Gump, "that's all I've got to say about that."

The hidden costs

Now before you go out and book an offsite hotel or something, let's talk about some of the other factors that might influence your decision - like the hidden costs of sleeping offsite.

> *But you just said it was cheaper to sleep offsite…*

That's not exactly what I said. Comparable class lodging is cheaper. BUT…

Yes, there is a big BUT there.

> *I have a big B…*

Stop it Pigment. We don't talk about that in mixed company.

> *Sorry!*

There are hidden costs to sleeping offsite. Let's look at a few of them.

Transportation

The biggest hidden cost of staying offsite is transportation. You have to somehow get to and from Walt Disney World.

If you stay in a Disney hotel, you can use Disney Transportation for your whole trip, even to and from the airport. For FREE.

Disney Transportation starts with Disney's Magical Express, a shuttle service to and from the Orlando airport. It's free to Disney Resort Hotel guests. You can land in Orlando and let Disney drive you around the whole trip and all the way back to the airport and it doesn't cost you any thing.

Think of the money you'll save. No rental car ($200+ per week). No taxis (at more than $70 each way to the airport), no parking fee at the parks (at $20 per day) or at the hotel (another $20 per night at some hotels), no gas… it adds up.

Yes, some of the hotels have shuttles that go to the parks on a set schedule. Some are close enough to walk to Disney Springs (though you can't get to the parks directly from there), but transportation is a major factor to consider when you are looking at staying offsite.

Another hidden cost is time. It's all about…

Location, location, location

Location, Location, Location. When you talk about Where to sleep, a really, really big consideration is location.

When Walt and his team started buying land in Florida, they bought a bunch. And then they tucked the Magic Kingdom at the furthest point from the entrance. They did that on purpose. They wanted to control what was around the park.

The result is that it's at least a 20-minute drive from any offsite hotel to the Magic Kingdom parking lot, and another 10 or more minutes to get to the park gate from there. And that's on a good day. On a bad day, that commute can reach a couple of hours.

Sleeping offsite can mean it takes significantly more time to get to the parks. And it's more challenging to go back to your hotel if you want to take a midday nap/swim break.

Even with sleeping onsite, location can play a part. If you sleep in one of the Monorail hotels, you can be at the Magic Kingdom in just a few minutes. Right at the gate. The Epcot Area Hotels are just a short walk or boat ride to both Epcot and Disney's Hollywood Studios.

The Monorail hotels and the Epcot Area Hotels are very convenient (but that does come with a higher price tag). You might want to consider that as you choose Where to Sleep.

Magic or annoying?

A major consideration when choosing Where to sleep is the Magic of Disney.

When you sleep at a Disney Resort, you are immersed in Disney Magic from the time you hear that first "Welcome Home" until that last "See Ya Real Soon." The walls, the bed, the shower, and everything else in the room, the lobby, and the pool have little Magical Disney touches. It's cute.

It's one of the reasons we keep going back. We love the cute Disney touches.

But, some people say it's annoying. I don't know who these people are. My guess is they've never actually stayed in a Disney resort or they are just "pinko commies" (a phrase from my youth).

Careful with the pink jokes.

I've put together a cool eBook about the hotels at Walt Disney World to help you get a glimpse of the style and amenities at each one.

SimpleFunMagic.com/Dads-Guide-To-Disney-Hotels

You might find it helpful.

The Where To Sleep Tool

Speaking of helpful tools, Dad has created a little Where to Sleep Tool to help you decide Where to sleep (Funny how that works). It will walk you through a series of questions and suggest the best options for your family. It's Simple, it's Fun, and it's kind of Magic.

Give it a try at:

SimpleFunMagic.com/Where-To-Sleep-Tool

Take your answers and add them to the Where to Sleep Worksheet.

SimpleFunMagic.com/The-Where-To-Sleep-Worksheet

By now you should know what's coming next. Yes, the sharing thing. Come on over and tell Dad Where you're going to sleep. I'd love to chat about it.

Dad's Bottom Line

Here's my take on the Where to sleep thing.

When you travel (to Disney or anywhere else), the one place you spend the most time in is Where you sleep. It's your home base. You are pretty much living there for the duration of your trip.

My thought is you get the best room you can afford. The biggest, the most convenient, the one that offers the most amenities, the one with the most Magic and the one you are most comfortable with. The one that fits your personality.

Because this trip is all about YOU! It's all about what YOU want, what YOU like, what YOU see... Oops. Slipping into the Toby Keith mode.

The Next Step

We've wrapped up Why, Who, When, and Where, and What. So next in the old English Class lesson comes the How?

> How? Like the Indian Chief* in Peter Pan? That How?

Not exactly, Pigment. Not exactly.

---

*The Indian Chief is a character in the 1953 Disney Animated Classic, Peter Pan. He is the father of Peter's love interest, Tiger Lily.

PLANES, TRAINS, OR AUTOMOBILES
HOW ARE YOU GOING TO GET THERE?

"Congratulations. Your Chevrolet Custom Concept vehicle
is ready for performance testing on the SimTrack."
- Test Track*

We've made our way through all the W questions. So that leaves us with the How question. Actually it's going to be two questions for the price of one:

- How are you going to get to Orlando?
- How are you going to get around once you get there?

Let's get started.

Planes, trains, and automobiles

Are you ready for an adventure? It's time to talk about How to get to Orlando. This one is usually a pretty easy question to answer, but let's go through the options, just for grins.

*Test Track is an interactive, high speed, automotive themed dark ride in Epcot's Future World.

Planes

One of the best ways to get to Walt Disney World is to fly to Orlando. Yes, in a plane. Yes, just like Dusty!

SimpleFunMagic.com/Meet-Dusty

Oh, I guess your plane might be a little bigger than Dusty.

When you think about How to get to Walt Disney World, coming in a plane is actually pretty Simple.

Orlando International Airport (MCO)

The Orlando airport is pretty unique as far as major airports go in that it's not dominated by one airline. All the major airlines fly into Orlando International and have a pretty robust schedule.

Orlando has one of the nicest, best run airports in the whole world. No, I'm not just spouting some Chamber of Commerce line. I have spent a lot of time in the Orlando airport (and with the Air Traffic Controllers there) and I can honestly say, it's the best-run airport I've been in.

I used to teach Air Traffic Controllers so I know a thing or two about how airports are run. And I can say without hesitation that the Orlando International Airport is run really well.

Be sure to stop by the main lobby during Christmas time and see the big Christmas Tree. It's just beautiful.

Orlando Sanford International Airport (SFB)

Be very careful when you are booking your airline tickets. Be careful of Sanford. No I'm not talking about Fred and Lamont (look that one up), I'm talking about Sanford, Florida.

There is an airport in Sanford, Florida that sometimes gets confused with the Orlando airport. But there is a really big difference between the Orlando International Airport (MCO) and the Sanford Airport (SFB).

A couple of "value" airlines fly into the Sanford airport. They do have some really cheap flights. It might be tempting to try one of those. You need to know that Sanford is about 50 miles from Walt Disney World.

You can't get Disney's Magical Express (Disney's free airport transportation system) from Sanford. Magical Express is only from Orlando International.

You will have to either rent a car from Sanford or spring for an alternate means of transportation.

FYI: A cab is over $100 ONE WAY from Sanford to WDW.

> *$100 just to get from the airport to Disney World? That's crazy!*

Yes it is Pigment. Yes it is.

Trains

I think Pixar's next movie needs to be called Trains. They've already done *Cars* and *Planes*. Can't you just see the movie poster now? Trains!

If you live on the East Coast, you can get to Walt Disney World by train. In fact, you can actually take a train to Florida and bring your car along.

> *Dad, you said we had to live on the East Coast. But I see that you can get to Orlando on train from just about anywhere.*

That's technically true, but did you see how long it takes and how much it costs? From Oklahoma City to Orlando you go to Fort Worth, then Chicago, then Washington DC, then to Orlando. It takes over 4 days and costs more than an airplane ticket.

> *Oh.*

Even going from Atlanta to Orlando involves a stop in Washington and takes over 32 hours in a train and a 5-hour layover in Washington. You could almost ride a bicycle faster.

But it's a nice 17-hour plus train trip from Washington to Orlando. That's not too bad and the cost isn't terrible (unless you want an actual bed to sleep in).

Then there is the whole "Auto Train" thing where your car can travel right along with you. The Auto Train (that's what Amtrak calls it) departs from Lorton, Virginia and goes to Sanford, Florida (yes, the same Sanford, Florida) and back every day.

What's more romantic than traveling by train? Not much. But, at what cost?

Automobiles

Around 66 million people visit Orlando every year. Only about 38 million fly into the Orlando International Airport, and not all of those are tourists.

My guess is a whole lot of people drive to Orlando. Duh. Probably more people come by car than by plane. It makes sense, as driving is "the American way," to quote my buddy Sam Eagle.*

Shoot, out here in Middle America, driving is a right of passage. We love our cars and spend a lot of time driving all over the place.

I am one of those drive-everywhere-guys. For three years I actually commuted 105 miles to work.

> Wow, Dad. That's a lot of driving, 105 miles per day.

Now, it was 105 miles each way, not per day. Yeah, I know, it sounds crazy. It's a long story that I won't bore you with, but let's just say… I like to drive myself around.

So what are the advantages and disadvantages of going to Walt Disney World by automobile?

Advantages of having a car at WDW

I could go on and on about the advantages of having a car at WDW. I talk about it all the time. But here are a few of the highlights of why you should

*Sam Eagle is an especially patriotic character featured in the Muppets franchise.

think about having alternate means of transportation and NOT let Disney do all the driving:

- **You are in charge** – Disney Transportation is great. It is. But it doesn't run on your schedule. It's not unusual to wait 20 minutes or more for a bus or Monorail or boat. At night when the kids are sleepy and you have to hold them standing in line for a bus or something it can get tiring. Just saying.

- **You can go off Disney property and eat at some of the less expensive options beyond WDW** – You can go to the store and get drinks and snacks and even food to cook. Or you can bring your own from home. Let's face it, food at Disney World is expensive and getting it offsite is a good way to save money.

- **There are a ton of other entertainment options around Orlando** – Having a car gives you the freedom to try some of them.

- **You can make the trip an experience** – We try to find stops along the way at interesting places like the battlefields in Vicksburg, the NASA engine testing facility in Mississippi, the battleship in Mobile and of course Lambert's Cafe – home of the Throwed Rolls.

Disadvantages

Let's talk about some of the disadvantages of going to Walt Disney World by automobile. Sorry, this one is going to be shorter.

- **The number one disadvantage of driving to Orlando is that it's tiring** – A Walt Disney World vacation is exhausting enough. It's like running a marathon every day. You don't want to be worn out before you even start. Or worse, have to do the return drive when you're all tuckered out.

- **It might not save you any money** – The last few trips we have "done the math"

to see about driving to Orlando and it was cheaper to fly. Lots cheaper. Gas, hotels along the way, meals, wear and tear on the car, it all added up and we ended up flying.

• **It takes time to drive** – Let's face it, if you live more than a couple of states away, it take a lot of time to drive to Florida. Even from the Florida state line it's another 2 hours or so to get to WDW at the shortest point and 8 hours or more from the Panhandle. For us here in Oklahoma, it's about 20 hours or more of driving. We can get there in a plane in 5 or so hours, even without a direct flight. If you have all the time in the world, driving is great. But if you have limited vacation time, do how much of it do you want to spend travelling?

• **You might not get to ride in one of the cool Minnie Vans*** – or enjoy other neat forms of transporation like the Monorail!

I love having a car at WDW. I love the freedom it offers, the control. I like Disney's transportation system, but if I have my way, I'm in a car driving myself.

Driving to Orlando is, OK, let's be honest here, it's not all that Fun. As much as I am a Midwestern US driving nut (and I am), a Walt Disney World vacation is tiring enough without adding a couple of extra days or more of driving.

OK, Worksheet time!

 SimpleFunMagic.com/The-How-To-Get-Around-Worksheet

Go ahead, Pigment is waiting…

Don't blame this on me!

So on to question two of our How series…

---

*Minnie Vans are a brand new program by Disney that uses cars decorated like Minnie Mouse to transport guests between destinations around Walt Disney World.

How are you going to get around once you get there?

Dad, what do you mean, "how am I going to get around when I get there?" Can't I just walk? I've been to Disneyland you can walk everywhere.

One of the big misconceptions about Orlando and Walt Disney World is how big it is and how spread apart everything is. It's 20 miles from the airport to WDW. Shoot, inside Walt Disney World itself, it's almost 5 miles from the Magic Kingdom to Epcot.

It's a $70+ dollar cab ride from Walt Disney World to the airport. One way. Don't ask me how I know that.

How do you know that?

I told you not to ask.

But since you asked I'll tell you:

OK, moving along. We need to spend a little time talking about the options for How to get around Orlando, and we're going to start by talking about taking a cab.

Take a cab

There are several cab services in Orlando. They do a great job of getting you from where you are to where you want to be. They can even get you around inside of Walt Disney World. You'll find cabs at all the major transportation areas.

The price for cabs is regulated by law and the charge is by the mile. It's about $65 to $70 to get from Walt Disney World to the airport and around $26 to get from the Pop Century to the Polynesian Village (my two favorite hotels at Walt Disney World).

Uber

Uber is the new kid on the block. It's everywhere and it's in Orlando. It's a lot cheaper than cabs. It costs between $25 and $55 dollars to Uber from WDW to the airport and between $7 and $25 to go from the Pop to the Polynesian.

Uber drivers sometimes aren't quite as quickly available as cabs (hotels and airports tend to have cabs lined up) so you should probably check the driver arrival time estimate on the Uber app and schedule your pickup location accordingly. And here's a bonus – the UberFamily option allows you to select a car with car seats if you need them!

Public transportation

There is public transportation in Orlando. There are 2 different Orlando public transportation services: LYNX and i-Ride. We'll skip i-Ride because it doesn't service the WDW area.

LYNX buses stop at the Transportation and Ticket Center and at Disney Springs. They run every 20 to 30 minutes from early in the morning until around midnight. Schedules vary so be sure to check golynx.com for more information.

The LYNX buses aren't always easy to use if you want to get to some of the other theme parks.

Huh? What do you mean by that?

Say you want to go to Universal Studios from Walt Disney World. I could say you can't get there from here, but according to the Google Maps (which the LYNX system uses for their route calculation) while you can get there with just one bus ride, it takes about an hour, and there is a catch: the bus stop is a mile and a half from Universal and you have to walk the rest of the way.

Also, it can take a while to get to the LYNX bus stops. Disney buses don't go from the hotels to the Transportation and Ticket Center. Also, getting to Disney Springs can be a challenge.

Each trip on LYNX is $2 regardless of distance or transfers (ask for a transfer ticket when you get off). You can buy a 7-day all access ticket for $16 per person.

Travel in style

One of the coolest ways to get around Orlando is by limo. No, I'm not kidding. It's cool.

> *A limo ride. I'm going on a limo ride. Can I get a drink in one of those cool looking glasses they have?*

As long as it's Diet Dr. Pepper…

When we went to Orlando with the whole family, I got the guys together and we planned a surprise for the families. THE PLAN called for us not to stray off Walt Disney World property, so we didn't need a rental car. I suggested that we rent a limo to and from the airport. So we did and we kept it secret from the families.

We booked a couple of limos (because we were coming in two groups.)

This was before Disney's Magical Express. Back then you had to find some way to get from the airport to WDW. It turned out getting a limo was cheaper than a shuttle for 15 people. So we took limos.

The surprise was priceless. The kids loved it. The wives loved it. Mrs. Mom's Mom almost cried. Actually she did cry.

There are all kinds of limo services in Orlando. They start at around $85 for a family of 4 from the airport to WDW.

Let Disney do the driving

Sit back, relax and let Disney do the driving. Shoot, they will even take care of your luggage. It's Magic!

Earlier I mentioned Magical Express to get to and from the airport. It's really cool and it's FREE!

Disney will happily chauffeur you around the resort for the rest of your trip. Disney's transportation is amazing. They have over 700 buses, a fleet of boats, and even 14 Monorails that move millions of people around the resort with surprising efficiency. It's one of the largest and best public transportation systems in the world.

Oh, and did I mention it's absolutely free?

Minnie Vans

Sometimes you need to get from Point A to Point B at Walt Disney World and there's no Simple way to get there. No longer.

For example, getting from say the Pop Century Resort to the Animal Kingdom Lodge for a meal at Boma or Jiko is not an easy task. In the past, there have been no direct Disney transportation options. Until now.

Disney has recently introduced Minnie Vans, which are Chevy Traverse vans decorated to look like Minnie Mouse, that will take you between Disney destinations inside Walt Disney World.

A Minnie Van ride costs $20 per trip. (Minnie Vans seat 6 and have 2 car seats if needed.)

Disney Skyliner

Construction has begun on a new Disney Transportation system called the Disney Skyliner. I can't wait for this one.

The Disney Skyliner is a gondola that will have stops at the Pop Century/ Art of Animation Resorts, the Caribbean Beach Resort, Disney's Hollywood Studios and Epcot.

Not a lot of details are out on the Disney Skyliner yet, but it looks COOL!

Rental car

I love driving myself. I think I mentioned that before. When we fly into Orlando, we almost always rent a car.

The rental car system at the Orlando Airport is one of the quickest and easiest around. For the major car companies, the cars are located right at the terminal so you don't have to get on a shuttle to take you to your car.

You go to the car counters that are located at the baggage claim area in Terminal A and then walk across the street to the pick up area. Very convenient.

Rental cars have competitive prices in Orlando. It's one of the cheapest destinations in the world for a rental car.

Don't forget to share How you're getting to (and getting around) WDW:

SimpleFunMagic.com/Share-The-How

Dad's Bottom Line

How you are going to get to Orlando is a big decision. It's important. How you are going to get around once you arrive is just as important.

Are you going to let Disney do all the driving? Where are you staying? Are you flying or driving? Do you plan to go offsite? Are you comfortable taking a cab/Uber/bus? These are the questions you'll need to consider as you decide How you're going to get to and around Orlando.

The Next Step

The Next Step is to put all the parts of this English lesson together and make some reservations.

Make reservations? It's about time.

Yes it is, Pigment. Yes it is.

MAKING RESERVATIONS
A STEP-BY-STEP GUIDE

"Be our guest! Be our guest! Put our service to the test!"
– Mickey's PhilharMagic*

Now we know Why you are going, Who's going, When you are going, Where you are going to eat, Where you are going to stay, and even How you're going to get there.

It might just be time to make a few reservations.
Do you have any reservations Pigment?

> *Yep Dad, I've got a bunch of reservations.*
> *Like reservations about your sanity,*
> *reservations about what to do next,*
> *reservations about…*

Not that kind of reservations, silly pig.

We're going to talk about room reservations,
ticket reservations, dining reservations, things like that.

*Mickey's PhilharMagic is a 4D show in Magic Kingdom's Fantasyland which features a number entitled "Be Our Guest" – performed by Lumiere from the 1991 Disney Animated Classic, Beauty and the Beast.

Oh, those reservations. Why didn't you say so? No, I don't have any of those reservations, Dad. Where do I get them?

That's a good question Pigment. Let's look.

When to make reservations

The first question we need to look at when talking about making reservations is When. When should you make them?

The Simple answer is: as soon as possible for most things.

As soon as you have a date for your trip, you should look and see if it's possible to make reservations.

When you can actually make reservations depends on what you are trying to make reservations for. It can range from 30 days before you arrive (FastPass+ if you aren't staying in a Disney hotel) all the way up to 499 days or more (for hotel reservations).

So let's break down the Who, What, When, Where, Why and How of making reservations.

Grab your "trip bible" – it's time to go to work.

The easy way...

The Simple (and, in my opinion, the best) way to make all your reservations is to turn it over to a highly trained professional. Yes, I know, Disney makes it easy to do it yourself, but that doesn't mean it's Fun!

I'm a big fan of using a GOOD Disney travel agent to make reservations. In fact, I believe a GOOD Disney travel agent can make the difference between a great trip and a Magical trip.

Even as "well versed" in Disney travel as I am, I still use a Disney travel agent every time I go to Walt Disney World (even the time I just went for one night). Let me tell you why.

SimpleFunMagic.com/Why-I-Use-A-Travel-Agent

A GOOD Disney travel agent will make things Simple. They help you with every step of your trip. They'll work with you to make your reservations (yes, even the dining and FastPass+ reservations). It will be Fun. They will help you with My Disney Experience, and they can even work some Magic with you on your itinerary.

I know the answer to this before I even ask, but, hey Dad, do you have a recommendation for a GOOD Disney travel agent.

I sure do Pigment. I'm glad you asked.

Like I had any choice.

I totally and completely recommend my friends and travel agent partners from Destinations to Travel. They make going to Walt Disney World Simple, Fun and Magic.

Trust me.

! SimpleFunMagic.com/Dads-Travel-Agent

PS. Destinations to Travel is a really GOOD Disney travel agency.

Dad's Bottom L---

STOP!!! Dad stop. You can't just say go to a travel agent to make reservations and not tell us how we can do it ourselves.

So, Pigment. Are you saying you want to ignore Dad's sage advice and book your trip all by yourself?

I just think you should at least tell how it could be done.

Mmmm, I guess I could do that.

Come on Dad, ole computer geek you. You love playing with webpages and telling everyone how they work. It'll be Fun.

OK, OK. I'll do it. Here…

Booking a Disney hotel

If you are planning to stay at a Disney hotel, here's how to book your whole Disney vacation.

Step 1
Go to the Walt Disney World website (disneyworld.com).

Step 2
Fill out the "Price Your Vacation" form at the top of the homepage.

Step 3
Follow the prompts to select your hotel, room type, ticket type, and more.

Step 4
Pay your money.

There. Are you satisfied now?

Now Dad. You're pouting. Stop it. There's a lot more to it than that.

Actually Pigment, it really is that Simple. You do go to Disney's website. You fill out the form on the front page. Then you follow the instructions. Pay your money and you're done.

That sounds pretty boring. Can you make it Fun?

That's a good idea, Pigment. To make it Fun and throw in a little Magic, I've created a web page where I walk you through each of the steps complete with screenshots and instructions.

That way if Disney changes anything we can update it to keep it current.

SimpleFunMagic.com/Make-Disney-Reservations

Oh, and you can book your hotel, tickets, dining plan, airline tickets, and even transportation options right on the Disney website.

As for When to book your hotel – like Dad said, as soon as you know you're going to Walt Disney World. But if you're staying in a Disney hotel, I strongly recommend you book before the 180 day mark – we'll get to why in the Advanced Dining Reservations section of this chapter.

Now can I do the Dad's Bottom Line thing?

NO!!!!! You're not done yet, Dad.

What? I told you the easy and best way to book everything. I've showed you how to book your vacation through Disney. What else do you want to know?

What about making those dining reservation things, FastPass+ reservations? What about buying Disney tickets not from Disney? What if I'm not staying at a Disney hotel?

There are about a thousand other things you need to talk about. Come on Dad. Get with it.

Man, you're pushy today, but if you insist…

Thank you!

I think I'm going to work backward on your list Pigment.

Whatever.

Non-Disney places to sleep

As I said back in the Where to Sleep chapter, it seems like there are about thirteen hundred and fifty two places to sleep around Walt Disney World. There are way too many to cover them all.

So I've picked a few of the more popular Where to sleep places and created a webpage that talks about making reservations at them.

SimpleFunMagic.com/Sleeping-With-The-Enemy

Buying Disney tickets

I think you mentioned Disney Tickets next.

> *Yes I did.*

If you aren't getting a discount based on tickets (a lot of Disney room or package discounts require a ticket purchase), you might want to buy tickets from someone other than Disney. It will save you some money.

You have to be very careful when buying park ticket from anyone other than Disney. Every year we hear stories of people who buy "cheap Disney tickets" that aren't any good.

You should always use an authorized vendor when buying tickets. For Disney tickets, use an authorized Disney ticket reseller. These are places that Disney has chosen to work with to sell tickets.

The authorized Disney ticket reseller I recommend is The Official Ticket Center.

! SimpleFunMagic.com/The-Official-Ticket-Center

So, When should you buy tickets? Whether you buy them as a part of a package or not, you should buy your tickets before you hit the 60 day mark if you're staying in a Disney hotel, or before the 30 day mark if you're staying off site. That has to do with FastPass+ reservations…

FastPass+

I'm going to skip FastPass+ for now. We haven't talked about it yet, what it is, how it's used, etc. We'll do that in the next section. I've got a whole bunch of good information about FastPass+ including how to make reservations.

Does that work, Pigment?

> *I suppose that will work just this once. But you still need to talk about dining reservations.*

You're right Pigment. I do. And I will. Right now.

It's about time.

Advanced Dining Reservations (ADRs)

Table Service and Signature Dining restaurants require reservations. Require might be a strong word, but for most of the restaurants it's true. You will have to have a reservation if you want to eat at most of the sit down restaurants at Walt Disney World.

Dad, you're repeating yourself.

I'm sorry, but it's important.

Plus, making ADRs can be Fun!

Um, Dad? What's an ADR?

Sometimes you ask the best questions Pigment.

Being Disney, a reservation can't just be called a reservation. For years, Disney wouldn't even use the term reservation when it came to dining, but a few years ago they finally gave in and coined the phrase Advanced Dining Reservations, or ADR.

Yes, I know ADR is an acronym and I hate acronyms but it is the term even Disney uses, so we'll call them ADRs too.

Like I said, for almost all of the sit down restaurants at Walt Disney World, you need an ADR.

I was talking to a friend who just got back from Walt Disney World. He was telling me about going to eat at one of the restaurants (I don't remember which one). He said they were walking by and decided to eat there. They went on the My Disney Experience app and found an ADR time 5 minutes away.

They made the reservation, and walked into the restaurant. As they came up to the podium they heard the greeter telling a lady that no, they didn't have any tables available for an hour and a half.

That should tell you something about how important making an ADR is.

Dad, you're making that up.

Nope. That's exactly what he said. Five (5) minutes, one and a half hours.

I will tell you for sure that at many of the restaurants, you won't get in without an ADR and they can be really hard to get.

So, Dad, how do I get one of these ADR things?

Another great question Pigment. You're on a roll. (I won't make the obvious roll joke about the pig on a roll when we're talking about dining.)

Thank you?

ADRs can be made 180 days prior to arrival day. At exactly 6am Eastern time your My Disney Experience account will allow you to make your ADRs for that day. You can do this no matter where you are staying or if you've even made your hotel reservations yet.

BUT, if you're staying in a Disney hotel (and have already booked your stay) you can book ADRs up to 10 more days. That gives you a good advantage in getting popular ADRs for later in your trip since you can book before the 180-day window opens for everyone else.

You can also call the Disney restaurants phone number (407) WDW-DINE at 7am Eastern time and make your reservations over the phone.

I highly recommend you make your dining reservations as soon as possible.

OK, Pigment. Did I cover everything?
Can I wrap it up now?

Yes you did Dad. Thank you.
You can do that Dad's Bottom Line
thingy now.

Thanks a bunch Pigment.

Dad's Bottom Line

Making reservations for your trip is Simple. It's Fun. It's Magic and it is exciting! Now it's getting real.

The Next Step

The Next Step is to take a little break and have some Fun as Dad talks about his Golden Rule.

Oh, that sounds like a really good time.

It will be, Pigment. It will be.

DAD'S GOLDEN RULE

**"I only hope that we don't lose sight of one thing
- that it was all started by a mouse"
-Walt Disney***

Now that we have that out of the way, I think it's high time we talked about Dad's Golden Rule.

Here's Dad's Golden Rule - Do unto others before they do unto you.

Wait a minute Dad. Isn't the Golden Rule, "Do unto others as you would have them do unto you"?

Yes it is. Very good Pigment. You get a gold star.
But Dad's Golden Rule is just a little different.
Let me explain.

Dad's Golden Rule is Simple, it's Fun and it's Magic!

A few months ago I was taking my normal

*Walt's referring to Mickey Mouse here, the lovable cartoon character that launched him to fame and fortune.

afternoon break from my exhausting Walt Disney World "research." I popped over to a local convenience store to grab a big Diet Dr. Pepper.

I'm kind of addicted to Diet Dr. Pepper which, by the way, is not available at Walt Disney World (very sad face emoji), but that's a whole other story.

When I walked into the store I saw my good friend, Bob. He was doing the same thing I was.

OK, he doesn't do exhausting Walt Disney World "research" but he was taking a break from his job and getting a soda, pop, Coke, or whatever you call it in your neck of the woods.

Bob is a very good friend (is that like redundant?) so, I walked over and said hello. We chatted for a minute and Bob left, then I went back to get my Diet Dr. Pepper.

When I went up to the counter to pay, the young lady behind the counter told me my buddy Bob had already paid for it. Now that put a smile on my face. How nice of Bob. He's a good guy.

Bob practiced Dad's Golden Rule. He did unto me before I could do it to him. (I got him back a few weeks later.) It was Simple. It was Fun. It was Magic. It put a smile right on my face. Thank you Bob!

Let's brainstorm about Dad's Golden Rule and Walt Disney World. What are some Simple pleasures, some Fun things, some Magical experiences that we can share with others at the Most Magical Place on Earth?

Try this one. A while ago, Disney changed the Disney Dining Plan to where you can share dining credits. So now you can pay for someone else's meal using your Disney Dining Plan.

There is nothing that will bring more Magic to a family than a server telling them oh, your meal is already paid for.

A friend of mine usually ends up doing a load or two of laundry at WDW to keep the suitcases light, and she makes sure to pack some extra laundry soap pods to leave in the laundry room with a little note for folks who've forgotten theirs.

That's a really Simple way to make a stranger's day.

A couple of other ways to implement Dad's Golden Rule are:

- Give up your spot in line or at a parade
- Get extra glow toys and share them at night
- Give away pins
- Make friends in line
- Make Thank You Cards and give them to Cast Members
- Tip MouseKeeping in creative ways
- Trade in extra Disney Dining Plan credits for candy and share it
- Wish people "happy-whatever-they-are-celebrating" on their buttons
- Take photos for others (but give the camera back)
- Sing "Let it go" all the time (OK this one might get annoying)

Jesus himself said, "It is more blessed to give than to receive." Who am I to argue with Jesus? Silly question.

When you practice Dad's Golden Rule you will be the one who is blessed. Trust me.

Want to talk more about Dad's Golden Rule and tell us some of your Simple, Fun, Magic ideas for sharing with others? Go over to our Share page, see what others are saying, and jump right in.

 SimpleFunMagic.com/Share-Dads-Golden-Rule

Dad's Bottom Line

Random acts of kindness are one of the easiest ways to put some Magic in your vacation, and will bless others. It's Fun, it's Simple and it's Magic for everyone!

The Next Step

So now it's time for the Fun section. It's time to head over to the parks.

Park? I love going to the park.
Can I play on the swing set? Wheeeeee!

Wrong park, Pigment. Wrong park.

FUN

It's time to have some Fun! This is really Dad's favorite part of the whole planning process.

Plan to conquer the theme parks

I'm going to help you become Hot STUFF by showing you how to create a PLAN to Conquer the Theme Parks at Walt Disney World.

I call it Section Fun.

In Section Fun, I'm going start by giving you some super secret rules for completing one of the hardest tasks in the whole world. Conquering the theme parks.

Please, (I'm talking to you Pigment) PLEASE don't leak these super secret rules to anyone because they won't work if everyone starts using them.

Me leak? What every makes you think I would leak?

Remember the Facebook debacle?

Oh, yeah that. I didn't think it would…
Oops, I mean, you never found out who did that. Did you?

F

I think I just did.

Sigh.

Next, we'll write YOUR PLAN for each park and more.

This is going to be Fun. Trust me. Here's what we're going to cover in Section Fun...

- Dad's 3 Simple Rules for becoming HOT STUFF
- How to conquer the Magic Kingdom
- Why Epcot is the hardest park to plan for
- A look at the best of Disney's Hollywood Studios
- Where to "talk" to the animals (spoiler: it's Animal Kingdom)
- Planning for the water parks, Disney Springs, and more
- Shopping at WDW

In each of the park chapters you'll find a Simple Fun Magic spreadsheet that will guide you through choosing which attractions you "must see" and which attractions you might want to skip.

These Simple Fun Magic Spreadsheets will be invaluable as you put together your final plan or as we call it, the Final Exam. Be sure to fill out the Worksheets and add them to your "trip bible."

Dad's Bottom Line

Section Fun is going to be Fun. Trust me. Dealing with the theme parks is the heart of any good PLAN for Walt Disney World.

The Next Step

Are you ready to find out how to become Hot STUFF?!

Hot STUFF sounds Fun Dad.

It sure does, Pigment. It sure does.

9

HOT, HOT, HOT, HOT STUFF
THE SECRET TO CONQUERING THE PARKS

"Ladies and Gentlemen - the backside of water."
- The Jungle Cruise*

Yep, it's time to sing again. Because now you are about to become HOT STUFF. Go ahead girls, take it away.

So... Dad. You've piqued my interest. How exactly are you going to make me into HOT STUFF?

Piqued. Nice word Pigment!

Yes it is, now answer the question.

Well... I'm going to stick an apple in your mouth.

Nooooooooo! Not that again. I hate it when that happens.

*The Jungle Cruise is a boat ride in Adventureland at Magic Kingdom.

Just kidding Pigment. Calm down and quit biting me.

Turn about is fair play right?

Let's move on.

Good idea.

Plan to conquer the theme parks

I'm going to help you become HOT STUFF by showing you how to create a PLAN to Conquer the Theme Parks at Walt Disney World.

I'm going to give to you (because I'm such a nice guy) some super secret rules for completing one of the hardest tasks in the whole world. This task is so hard that there are only 10 people who have ever really mastered it (I'm just guessing at that number, and I'm probably on the high end).

Dad is HOT STUFF

Way back in around 1986, Mrs. Mom and I went to Walt Disney World. News Flash: Dad went to WDW.

We interrupt this book to bring you the following special announcement. A normal guy and his wife from Oklahoma left their 18-month-old child at home and went to Walt Disney World.

Big deal Dad. Whoopee.

It was a big deal to us Pigment.
"Normal guy..." that was a low blow.

This was actually the first time I went as a Dad and Mrs. Mom as a mom. The Princess was about 18-months-old at the time and I badgered Mrs. Mom into leaving her with the family (she was a great baby) and taking an "after-the-babymoon" to Walt Disney World.

Now you've got to remember that this was before the Internet days. Shoot, this was even before Dad got his total obsession with Disney. (Right.)

One evening we were walking through Epcot. We'd had a great day but we needed something to cap it off.

Then IT happened. Dad became HOT STUFF. King of the Lab (for you Bones lovers). That night, Dad became the Conquering Hero of Epcot.

Oh, come on. Get your minds out of the gutter ladies. Dad's a straight-laced, tee-totaling, Bible-Belt-living, clean-cut, Christian man.

So what did Dad do to become HOT STUFF?

Dad convinced Mrs. Mom that IT was all part of his PLAN. Winner, Winner, Chicken Dinner.

As we were walking through Epcot in the afternoon, I happened to notice a sign over on the American Gardens Theater that talked about IT. IT was happening later in the evening. I had found IT. Now all I had to do was to get Mrs. Mom back to IT when it was time for IT.

Remember, like I said before, this was before the Internet, before every Peter, Paul and Mary wrote a book about Walt Disney World. Walt Disney World information just wasn't available back then.

And I had found IT.

IT was amazing. IT made me the Conquering Hero. The King of the Lab. IT made me HOT STUFF.

Boy that's a lot of "ITs" Dad. You ever going to share what "IT" was?

IT was a concert by none other than Toni Tennille. Google her. She was big time in our day. And right in the middle of her concert her husband came out and the show really started.

SimpleFunMagic.com/Love-Will-Keep-Us-Together

Yes, Dad sang loud. (Dad sings good.)

Mrs. Mom was so thrilled with IT she proclaimed, right then and there, that Dad was HOT STUFF, King of the Lab, and, you guessed it, the Conquering Hero of Epcot.

(OK, so maybe that's not exactly what she said, but she was pretty happy and so was I.)

Maybe IT was just dumb luck, but Dad had found the perfect ending to the perfect day. And it started Dad down the path of becoming the world's greatest Walt Disney World trip planner. Oh, and he's really HOT STUFF too.

So, Dad. That's a cute little story, but, how are you going to make me King of the Lab? HOT STUFF? The Conquering Hero of Walt Disney World?

Little? LITTLE? Where's that apple…

NOOOOOO!!!!

Instead, check this out. Here's what we're shooting for:

SimpleFunMagic.com/How-Its-Done

You made me do it. (Or maybe that was the devil.)

Somebody call for a devil?

OK, enough vamping. Let's get to this.

Dad's 3 Simple Rules

What I'm going to do is to teach you how to create a PLAN that will Conquer the Theme Parks. It's pretty Simple. Yep, it's going to be Fun and DUH, it's Walt Disney World, it's bound to be Magic.

First, let me introduce you to **Dad's 3 Simple Rules for Conquering the Theme Parks at Walt Disney World.**

Yes, Just 3 Rules. Here they are —

DAD'S 3 SIMPLE RULES
FOR CONQUERING THE THEME PARKS
AT WALT DISNEY WORLD

1 ▸ Get to the parks early

1A ▸ Have a PLAN

2 ▸ Ride the "busy" rides first

3 ▸ Figure out how to master FastPass+

I never said I could count.

That's it. It's all you need to know. Now YOU can now go out and be HOT STUFF, King of the Lab and the Conquering Hero.

Trust me.

Chapter done. Dad's so good!

> *Dad, that was pretty underwhelming. Would you mind expanding on those rules a little bit?*

What? You want more? OK, I guess…

Here's what we'll do. First, I'll explain the Rules and how to apply them. Then we'll look at each of the parks. How does that sound?

> *Good. Finally. Meat on the bone. Get to it!*

Meat on the bone. That's pretty Funny coming from you, Pigment. Here we go.

Get to the parks early

Rule I – Get to the Parks Early – this is the most basic, the most important, the most time savingest rule you'll ever see. I can't say enough about getting to the Parks first thing in the morning.

Here's how the crowd patterns work at Walt Disney World. It doesn't matter what day, what week or what year. This pattern always follows.

Every day? Even Christmas?

Yes, Pigment. Even Christmas.

When the park opens there aren't any crowds. Then the park fills for the next few hours until there's a peak in the crowd levels sometime in the late afternoon.

As the evening progresses the crowds slowly dissipate until the park closes and Disney starts running everyone out.

OK, maybe on Christmas Day when the Magic Kingdom closes to new guests at 10am, the pattern doesn't completely hold, or maybe a big afternoon thunderstorm that sends people fleeing, but for 300 or more days a year, you can count on Rule I.

Now here's something we haven't discussed yet: **Extra Magic Hours.**

Extra Magic WHAT?!

Extra Magic Hours. It's a pretty cool perk, and it's Simple to use. It can add hours of Fun to your trip, and a lot of Magic. Here's what you need to know:

If you are a Disney resort hotel guest, you can take part in Extra Magic Hours. Every day, one of the 4 theme parks will either open one hour early or stay open a couple hours late just for Disney hotel guests. This means that you can spend time in the parks going on rides with fewer people – your waits will be shorter and a lot of the time you'll have no wait at all! How cool is that?

Extra Magic Hours are published with park hours about 6 months in advance, so you can incorporate them into your PLAN. If you can get up extra early or stay up super late, these can really help you become HOT STUFF.

Have a PLAN

Rule 1A – Have a PLAN – there is nothing sadder than watching a family walk down Main Street about 2pm in the afternoon, stop half way, right in the middle of the street. Pull out a map and say, "where are we going to start?" Or even worse, to ask, "which way to Spaceship Earth?"

A PLAN is a thing of beauty. It is calming. It gives purpose. It keeps everyone in line. OK, maybe that's going a little far, but A PLAN is a good thing.

We've talked pretty much ad nauseam about having A PLAN so I'll quit beating it up except to say that you need one (yes, more to come on the specifics).

Ride the busy rides first

Rule 2 – Ride the "busy" rides first – this is a corollary to Rule 1. Because the lines are shorter in the morning, ride the "busy" rides first because the lines will be shorter (Dad's a genius when it comes to this logic stuff).

Dad, what are these so-called "busy rides?"

I'm glad you asked:

SimpleFunMagic.com/The-Busy-Rides

Rule 2 is meant to be used in conjunction of all the other rules. It is dependent on Rule 1. If you arrive in a park in midafternoon, Rule 2 won't work. It also works better if you have a Rule 1A: A PLAN. You also choose which "busy" rides YOU want to go on based on Rule 3 and if you have a FastPass+ reservation already…

You get the picture.

Use FastPass+

Rule 3 – Figure out how to use FastPass+. When Disney revamped FastPass a couple of years ago and introduced FastPass+. FastPass+ (yes, that is typed correctly Disney loves smashing two words together) became the most powerful planning tool ever imagined. Now you can schedule your time to be at a ride and be almost guaranteed of a short line.

Using FastPass+ correctly is a bit of an acquired skill. Yes, you can open up My Disney Experience and make random reservations, but the skill comes in planning times to match when you are in the vicinity of the ride. That takes years of practice, dedication and training. Or just some old fashioned dumb luck.

Just kidding. FastPass+ is pretty much common sense, and it all depends on the other Rules.

We have a cool guide to FastPass+. Go over and look at it:

SimpleFunMagic.com/Dads-Guide-To-FastPass

Dad's Guide to FastPass+ lays out which rides you should get a FastPass+ reservation for and how to do it.

After you make YOUR PLAN and complete the Final Exam, you'll know where you plan to be and when – and that makes choosing which attractions and which times to make your FastPass+ reservations for a breeze.

But Dad, WHEN can I make FastPass+ reservations? Right now? On the fly?

Don't get too worked up Pigment. If you are a Disney hotel guest, you can make your FastPass+ reservations at 60 days out, and everyone else can make them at 30 days out (as long as you already have your tickets bought and linked to your My Disney Experience account). If you're buying your tickets at the gate, you can make them the same day of your visit, though the pickins will be slim.

There's nothing slim about me.

You said it, not me.

Dad's Bottom Line

There. Now you know how to be The Conquering Hero, The King of the Lab, HOT STUFF! Trust me on this. Follow these Simple rules and you will have Fun. You'll be shocked by the Magic that just falls into place.

The Next Step

Next Step is to talk about YOUR PLAN to Conquer the... drum roll please... The Magic Kingdom (said with total awe).

The Magic Kingdom! I LOVE The Magic Kingdom!!!!!!!!!

Me too, Pigment. Me too.

CONQUERING THE MAGIC...
MAGIC KINGDOM PLAN

"Welcome to our Unbirthday Party...
To spin your teacup, just turn the silver wheel to the right or to
the left. The faster you turn it, the faster it spins. It seems like
our ride is about to begin. Have the most wonderful time!"
- The Mad Tea Party*

In the movie Pinocchio, Jiminy Cricket sings the song "When You Wish
Upon a Star."

It's such a good song that Disney took it and built a whole fireworks show
around it**.

Oh, how I miss Wishes. It was sad to see it go. And such a great thought.
All I have to do is wish upon a star and my dreams will come true. If only
it were so.

*Hey, Dad, Wishes was great, but it seems like you're veering off the rails a
bit here. What on earth does wishing upon a star have to do with creating
a plan for Conquering the Magic Kingdom?*

*The Mad Tea Party is a spinning tea cup attraction in Fantasyland in Magic Kingdom, inspired
by the 1951 Disney Animated Classic, Alice in Wonderland. **That fireworks show was called
Wishes: A Magical Gathering of Disney Dreams and it ran from 2003-2017 at Magic Kingdom.*

OK, Pigment, we're this far into this book and you're still worrying that Dad can't take the most innocuous thing and make it fit the topic at hand? Watch and learn.

If you say so...

What were we talking about?

Magic Kingdom. Plan. Wishes. Rules...

A lot of people that go to Magic Kingdom are on the "Wishes" PLAN. They arrive on Main Street and wish upon a star that everything will be perfect.

These are the people that think they will have Magic Kingdom to themselves. All the characters will line Main Street just to greet them. The Monorail runs from their hotel door right to Cinderella Castle. Dole Whips flow from the water fountains, unicorns guide them to from ride to ride, and at last there is world peace. (There must be a John Lennon song in there somewhere.)

I can see it, Dad. I can see it flowing from the fountains. Dole Whip. Slurp, slurp...

Wake up Pigment. While this is a great dream, it's not reality.

Magic Kingdom, more than any other park, is the park where you need a PLAN. A PLAN. Not a Wishes, Dole Whips and unicorns PLAN, but a REAL, thought out, step-by-step PLAN.

And with a real PLAN you will be the King of the Lab, The Conquering Hero, Hot STUFF!

Dad's PLAN for Magic Kingdom

There is no disputing the fact that Magic Kingdom is the world's BEST theme park. Yep, I just said it, and you can't dispute it. I've decreed Magic Kingdom is the best and that makes it final.

This book thing going to your head a little Dad?

Check this out…

Twenty million.

What about 20 million? That's a big number.

Around 20 million people per year visit Magic Kingdom. That's an average of over 56,000 people per day. Every day. Three hundred and sixty-five or sixty-six days per year.

56,000 per day?

Yep. FIFTY-SIX THOUSAND people every day.

SimpleFunMagic.com/Theme-Park-Statistics

Wow. That's a lot of people.

That means the wait times in the lines at Magic Kingdom can be stunning. Even on slow days. It's not unusual for the mountains (Space Mountain, Splash Mountain and Big Thunder Mountain Railroad) to show waits of an hour or more on a SLOW crowd day.

OK, rambling again, Dad. Button it up.

Magic Kingdom is special. It is the best park in the world. It's also the one that can be the most frustrating without a real PLAN.

So let's talk about a PLAN for Magic Kingdom.

Finally.

The good news about Magic Kingdom is that it's really easy to make a PLAN to conquer. Actually, you might say it's Simple to plan for Magic Kingdom. It's Fun, and, if you do it right, it's Magic.
Somehow I knew you were going to say something like that.

Are you ready to be impressed?

There's a first time for everything.

Dad's Simple Fun Magic Guide to YOUR PLAN for Magic Kingom

Step 1 - Pick a land to start in. Ride the busy rides in that land.

Step 2 – Determine the direction you would like to go and work your way around the park riding the busy rides in each land. For the second lap, do everything you missed on the first lap.

Step 3 – Execute.

Done.

Now that was Simple, wasn't it?

I told you to be ready to be impressed. Dad is big time.

No, I'm not kidding. It really is that Simple.

> *Now wait just a doggone minute! I think that this Simple thing has gone to your head. It can't be that Simple. Can it? Pick a land to start in; determine what direction you want to move in; execute? There's got to be more to it than that. Really Dad? Really?*

OK, there's a little bit more to it. But not much.

Let's take those step-by-step.

Pick a land to start in

When we tour Magic Kingdom we always start out in Tomorrowland. It's kind of our thing. We love Tomorrowland, and we love starting our day with our favorite rides.

We'll ride the busier rides in Tomorrowland (Space Mountain, Buzz Lightyear's Space Ranger Spin, and Astro Orbiter) then make our way over to Fantasyland.

Again, busy rides (maybe with FastPass+ for Peter Pan's Flight or Seven Dwarfs Mine Train) and move on.

And so on, through Liberty Square (Haunted Mansion), Frontierland (Big Thunder Mountain Railroad and Splash Mountain), and Adventureland (Pirates of the Caribbean and the Jungle Cruise). Oh, I almost forgot...

PS: Remember Dad's 3 Simple Rules for Conquering the Theme Parks at Walt Disney World! (Boy, do we ever need to work on the names we give stuff.)

Dad's Simple Rules are the key to YOUR PLAN for Magic Kingdom.

Rule I – Get to the park early. Rule I is so important at Magic Kingdom, Disney prodded Dad to create a challenge just to prove this rule.

A few years ago (when Disney first introduced the concept of FastPass+), Disney said that the average guest visits 9 attractions in the Magic Kingdom per day.

Nine. 9. Five plus 4. Eight plus 1. In a 12 hour, or more, day. Less than one per hour. That's just nuts.

I believed that with a good Rule I, you could accomplish 9 attractions by noon. Thus **Dad's Nine By Noon Challenge** was born.

I don't want to spend a lot of time here talking about it, but let's just say that I was right. You can accomplish 9 attractions by noon. That's the power of getting to the parks early.

The same 9 attractions you can do in 3 hours in the morning will take you 6-8 hours in the afternoon/evening.

SimpleFunMagic.com/Nine-By-Noon

Dad's Nine by Noon Challenge is all about being at Magic Kingdom early and making the best use of your time during the day.

Rule IA – Have a PLAN – I think we've covered that one already.

Rule 2 – Ride the busy rides first – this one is absolutely, incredibly (I'm running out of adjectives) important in Magic Kingdom. The difference between the line length at 10am and 2pm is unbelievable.

SimpleFunMagic.com/The-Busy-Rides

Make two laps around the park. The first lap, in the morning, you are riding the busy rides first, the second lap to finish everything up.

Rule 3 – FastPass+. Yes, you need to know how to use FastPass+ in Magic Kingdom. I said it in the HOT STUFF chapter, and I'm saying it again. If you haven't read Dad's eBook yet, check it out:

SimpleFunMagic.com/Dads-Guide-To-FastPass

That's great Dad. Very helpful. I have one more quick question.

OK, I'm a bit scared, but go ahead.

There are a lot of rides, shows and things at the Magic Kingdom. How am I going to see them all?

Wow. That's a really, really good question Pigment. The quick answer is… you won't. Before you get all huffy, let me explain.

Way back in the first section of the book I talked about how we all are different. We all like different things. Me, I'm not a fan of things that go round and round so I avoid rides like The Mad Tea Party*.

You probably won't have time to experience every ride, show, or gift shop in the Magic Kingdom so you have to pick and choose which ones are most important to you.

So how do I do that?

I can help…

SimpleFunMagic.com/I-Can-Help

The Mad Tea Party is an attraction based on the birthday party scene in the movie "Alice in Wonderland." You ride around in spinning "tea cups."

Dad's Rate A Ride Spreadsheet

I'm kind of a techy, geeky guy and several years ago I decided I'd build a little tool for the family to help us choose what we would do on our Walt Disney World trips.

I built a spreadsheet with every ride, every show, every restaurant at Walt Disney World. Each member of the family would take the spreadsheet and rate everything from 0 to 5.

When everyone filled it out it, I totaled up the scores and it became obvious what we should do and what we should skip. There was a definite separation. It was pretty incredible.

I've taken that spreadsheet and updated it and made it into something everyone can use to choose what to do at Magic Kingdom.

Check it out…

SimpleFunMagic.com/Rate-A-Ride-Magic-Kingdom

Planning is not a Solo Sport

Remember, planning is not a Solo Sport. The Rate-a-Ride Spreadsheet is meant to be shared with all your travel party. All of them. Have everyone fill it out then look to see which attractions get the highest scores.

Those are the attractions you should have in YOUR PLAN.

Dad's Bottom Line

I'm serious. Making a Magic Kingdom PLAN is pretty easy.

Magic Kingdom is so well laid out that you can pretty much start in one land and work your way around the Castle. It's really that Simple.

Remember, this is YOUR PLAN for Magic Kingdom. Own it. Enjoy it. Have Fun with it.

The Magic is just a few steps away.

The Next Step

Now it's time to talk about the hardest of the WDW theme parks to plan for. Yep, I said the hardest.

Can you guess which one it is?

> *It's not Magic Kingdom… is it Blizzard Beach?*

Patience, Pigment. Patience.

THE HARD PARK
EPCOT PLAN

"We've gathered here tonight around the fire,
as people of all lands have gathered for thousands of years
before us, to share the light and share the story."
- IllumiNations: Reflections of Earth*

Ding. Ding. Ding… The winner is… You got it. Epcot.

What? Have you already forgotten? At the end of the last chapter I asked what is the hardest Walt Disney World Theme Park to plan for? The answer is… Epcot.

Epcot?

Yes, Epcot. What, did I stutter?

OK, Dad. That's an interesting answer. Why not (insert one of the other theme parks here)?

Are you questioning me? Don't you know who I am? Why I oughta…

*IllumiNations: Reflections of Earth is a nightly show on World Showcase Lagoon in Epcot which features pyrotechnics, lasers, fireworks, and more.

Just kidding.

There are three reasons Epcot is the hardest park for planning.

First, and most important, it's the hardest to get from Point A to Point B. There aren't any shortcuts, and everything is a mile or so apart (OK, that may be a bit of an exaggeration, but not much).

Second, Epcot is two parks in one. It's like Disney took two completely separate theme parks and just them threw them together.

Oh, yeah. That's exactly what they did (I'm not kidding).

Third, the lines at Epcot are long and boring. Disney didn't put a lot of thought into the queues (except for Test Track, and it's not as good as it used to be). I hate standing in line, and Epcot really does have the worst lines (maybe because there are relatively few "rides").

And finally, the World Showcase isn't all that appealing to kids. There, I said it. I know you were thinking it.

But Dad, you said three reasons.

Yes I did. I just threw the 4th one in as a bonus. Do I get a gold star?

NO!!! Dad, did you really just throw Epcot under the bus?

UNDER THE BUS? Wait just a doggone minute. I'm not throwing Epcot under the bus!

I love Epcot! I do.

Where else can you take a 2.5g rocket to Mars and ride down the Rivers of China, then walk over and grab a pizza with ingredients fresh from Naples, Italy (not Florida) and get a French crepe for dessert then see where Disney grows the food you just ate, and then talk to Crush* himself? It's kewl dude! (Whew. Take a breath Dad.)

Crush is a sea turtle who appears in the Pixar films Finding Nemo and Finding Dory. You can find him in the Turtle Talk with Crush attraction at The Seas with Nemo & Friends in Epcot's Future World.

All in one day.

Only at Epcot.

I love Epcot! I love Epcot! I LOVE EPCOT!

Is that better?

> A little.

So, now that we've established that I really do love Epcot, I'll make the point again…

Let's face it. The World Showcase isn't real kid friendly. They've tried to Fun it up, but…

SimpleFunMagic.com/How-Boring-Is-Epcot

OK, now that we've got all that out of the way… I love Epcot, let's get started on YOUR PLAN for Epcot.

Dad's Simple Fun Magic Guide to YOUR PLAN for Epcot

Here we go. Dad's Simple Fun Magic Plan for Epcot.

Step 1 - FastPass+, FastPass+, FastPass+ make a PLAN

Step 2 - Epcot is two parks. Do Future World first, World Showcase second.

Step 3 - Execute!

Done - You are getting good at this.

> But Dad! But Dad! But Dad!

WHAT?

> That sounds awfully Simple. Make FastPass+ reservations. Do Future World first then the World Showcase? Do I really treat the Epcot as two parks?

Yes, Epcot is that Simple. Let's break each of those down a little.

Put your plan together for FastPasses. Epcot has a Funky "tier" system for FastPass+ that makes it a little tricky, but not too bad. Make a FastPass+ Plan. Don't forget Dad's Ultimate Guide to FastPass+.

SimpleFunMagic.com/Dads-Guide-To-FastPass

Do Future World first, then World Showcase. Duh, the World Showcase doesn't even open until 2 hours after Future World. If you arrive at opening time, and head to World Showcase you're going to be pretty lonely.

Next, You really don't want to be jumping back and forth between Future World and World Showcase.

Epcot isn't like the other parks. With the lagoon in the World Showcase, you can't just hop from land to land like, say, the Magic Kingdom. It's a significant walk to anywhere.

That's why you'll want to separate the two and treat them as 2 parks. And you don't even need a Park Hopper!

Execute. Do it. Get 'er done. That's it. Drop the mic.

The Big 4

I do have to mention the Big 4?

> *Since no one has a clue what you're talking about it would probably be a good idea.*

Epcot has 4 attractions that have crazy long lines at times. If you can get through the Big 4 with a minimum wait then you will be the Conquering Hero, King of the Lab, and some really Hot STUFF!

The Big 4 are Soarin', Test Track, Mission Space and Frozen Ever After. Those are the attractions that have the longest lines at Epcot. If you conquer the Big 4, you conquer Epcot.

> *So, Dad, how do you handle the Big 4?*

Me, I would make a FastPass+ for either Test Track or Frozen Ever After (you can only choose one of those from that tier). Then as soon as the park opens I'd do the other one I didn't get a FastPass+ for, then Soarin' (that's in the same tier as the other two, so no FastPass+ here) and Mission Space (that's in a different tier, so you can get a FastPass+ if you want to) – in that order.

That would get through the Big 4 with the least time in line.

Dad, I hate to keep interrupting, but you didn't say anything about that confusing 3/4 rules thing. Do those work in Epcot? I thought you said they work at all the parks.

Yes Pigment. Dad's 3 Simple Rules for Conquering the Theme Parks at Walt Disney World do work in Epcot. In fact, they are crucial. Check this out.

Rule 1 – Get to the park early. Check. It works. Every time.

Rule 1A – Have a plan. You always need a plan.

Rule 2 – Ride the Busy rides first. That's the Big 4 thing.

SimpleFunMagic.com/The-Busy-Rides

Rule 3 – Know how to use FastPass+. That's Step 1.

Yep, Dad's 3 Simple Rules for Conquering the Theme Parks at Walt Disney World work for Epcot.

Is that all? It seems like there should be a little more.

OK, how about another of Dad's Rate-a-Ride Spreadsheets for Epcot?

Oooh, that will work!

SimpleFunMagic.com/Rate-A-Ride-Epcot

Just like I said last chapter, have everyone fill the Spreadsheet out and you'll know exactly what should be in YOUR PLAN for Epcot.

Dad's Bottom Line

Epcot is Fun. Planning for Epcot is sort of hard, but not really. Just figure out how to conquer the Big 4 and the rest will be easy.

The Next Step

The Next Step is to go to the movies…

Why don't you ever take me to a movie Dad?

Mmmm. Let me think? Grown man with a pig at the movie theater…

Oh. Yeah.

THE BEST WHAT?!
DISNEY'S HOLLYWOOD STUDIOS PLAN

"Hey wait a minute. We can't leave these people here like this."
- Rock 'n' Roller Coaster Starring Aerosmith*

Disney's Hollywood Studios (or whatever they're calling it this week**) has the best attractions at WDW. The Best!

No, I'm not kidding. Yes, the Magic Kingdom is my favorite, but Disney's Hollywood Studios has THE BEST attractions! Take it away guys…

No, it's not one of the "Fab 5***" but wow, it's a great song.

For me, that's the way I feel about Disney's Hollywood Studios. I don't want to miss a thing. Just look at this list:

*Rock 'n' Roller Coaster Starring Aerosmith is a high-speed indoor rollercoaster at Disney's Hollywood Studios set to music by the band Aerosmith. **In 2016, Disney announced that the name of Disney's Hollywood Studios would change for the third time. As of the writing of this book, the new name has not yet been revealed. ***The Fab 5 is what Dad calls the 5 Aerosmith songs that play in the cars on Rock 'n' Roller Coaster Starring Aerosmith.

Toy Story Mania!, The Twilight Zone Tower of Terror, Rock 'n' Roller Coaster Starring Aerosmith, Star Tours – The Adventures Continue, Muppet*Vision 3D, Indiana Jones Epic Stunt Spectacular!, Star Wars Launch Bay, Storm Troopers* patrolling the park...

But Dad, isn't everything closed at Hollywood Studios. I hear everyone say, "it's a dead park, a half-day park." They say "it's not worth it to even go."

Are you paying attention, Pigment?

I think so.

Did you see that list of the rides in DHS? (Yes, I'm getting lazy and abbreviating. My fingers hurt from all the typing. So from time to time in this chapter you are going to see DHS when I mean Disney's Hollywood Studios.)

And that's not even the whole list. There's Beauty and the Beast –Live on Stage, For the First Time In Forever: A Frozen Sing-Along, Voyage of the Little Mermaid, Fantasmic!, Disney Junior Live on Stage!, Jedi Training Academy, Mickey and Minnie Starring in Red Carpet Dreams, seasonal shows, and you sure don't want to miss the Star Wars: A Galactic Spectacular fireworks!

Half-day park? Closed? Dead? Not worth it? That's crazy talk!

In fact, on our last visit, Mrs. Mom and I spent from opening to closing in the park, and we still didn't see everything. There's plenty to see and do in DHS.

Oh, and I can't wait for all of the new stuff to open. I'll be like a kid at Christmas. But even now, DHS is a great park to visit.

New stuff? What new stuff?

Stuff like Star Wars Land (scheduled to open in 2019) and Toy Story Land

---

*Storm Troopers are the military troops for the "dark side" aka: the bad guys in the Star Wars franchise.

(slated to open in summer 2018). Nothing important. Just kidding. It's going to be cool.

Can we get on to the planning Dad?

Good idea.

Let's get started with YOUR PLAN for Disney's Hollywood Studios.

Dad's Simple Fun Magic Guide to YOUR PLAN for Disney's Hollywood Studios

Step 1 – Work outward in concentric circles, starting at the seventh radii of the third segment continuing until...

What?

Just kidding.

What I meant to say is break the park up into **5 Scenes**:

- Scene 1 – Sunset Blvd
- Scene 2 – Animation Courtyard and Pixar Place
- Scene 3 – Echo Lake and Hollywood Boulevard
- Scene 4 – Muppet Courtyard and Commissary Lane
- Scene 5 – Closing Shows

Step 2 – Prioritize the Scenes and make your FastPass+ reservations based on your priorities.

Proceed smoothly through the Scenes in your order.

Step 3 – Execute

As with the Magic Kingdom and Epcot, Dad's 3 Simple Rules for Conquering the Theme Parks at Walt Disney World are truly helpful here.

You've forgotten already? OK, here's a reminder.:

DAD'S 3 SIMPLE RULES
FOR CONQUERING THE THEME PARKS
AT WALT DISNEY WORLD

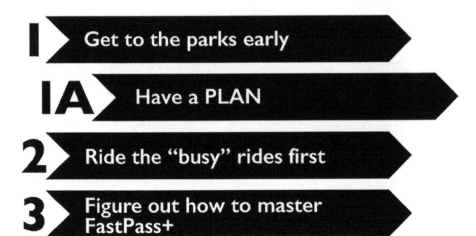

1 Get to the parks early

1A Have a PLAN

2 Ride the "busy" rides first

3 Figure out how to master FastPass+

While we're playing the reminder game, who knows what the ONE BIG TRUTH is?

Say it with me...

YOU'RE GOING TO WALT DISNEY WORLD!

Ding, ding, ding. That's right. You're going to Walt Disney World! This is going to be Fun. You can do this.

So to be the King of the Lab, the Conquering Hero of Disney's Hollywood Studios, and some really big Hot STUFF you need a good PLAN for how to conquer the Studios.

The first part of that plan is to figure out which attractions your travel party wants to experience. Yes, all of them. That's where Dad's Rate-a-Ride Spreadsheet for Disney's Hollywood Studios comes in. You know the drill by now. Download it. Pass it around and fill it out.

SimpleFunMagic.com/Rate-A-Ride-DHS

Fill out the Spreadsheet, and stick them in your "trip bible." We'll talk about it more later. Need a hand with figuring out what those busy rides are?

SimpleFunMagic.com/The-Busy-Rides

Dad's Bottom Line

Disney's Hollywood Studios has the BEST rides of all the Walt Disney World Theme Parks. The best. Heading into DHS without a PLAN is like going to Walmart to buy a car.

It's silly. It will make for a long day, especially when planning for DHS is so easy. You can do this. You can be the Conquering Hero, the King of the Lab, and we already know you're Hot STUFF!

The Next Step

Next, we had over to Animal Kingdom. Time to talk to the animals at the most unique theme park in the world.

> I like talking to the animals. Do you know what the tiger said to the elephant the last time we went on the Safari?

I'm afraid to ask, Pigment. I'm afraid to ask.

I LOVE TO TALK TO THE ANIMALS
ANIMAL KINGDOM PLAN

"Jambo!"
- Cast Members in Animal Kingdom*

That brings us to the last of the theme parks. Animal Kingdom. The easiest park to PLAN for if you know the one big secret.

The Most Uniquest Theme Park In The World

Animal Kingdom is the most uniquest Theme Park in the whole world.

*Dad, did you just say uniquest?
Is that a real word?*

Probably not, but it's my word, and it's exactly what Animal Kingdom is. The uniquest park in the world. In the whole world.

If you say so…

Jambo means "Hello" in Swahili, and it's a greeting frequently used by Cast Members in Animal Kingdom, particularly in the Africa area of the park.

Nahtazu

Animal Kingdom is different. Animal Kingdom is part theme park and part zoo (just don't tell Disney I called it a zoo).

A long time ago, back when Animal Kingdom opened, Disney ran Nahtazu commercials for several years. Hey Disney, we get the picture, but...

Yes, Disney, Animal Kingdom is a zoo. A really cool zoo. The best zoo anywhere, but it's still a "zu."

Nahtazu is by far the biggest park at WDW.

> *Not Magic Kingdom?*

Nope, not Magic Kingdom, not Epcot, not Disney's Hollywood Studios. The biggest park at Walt Disney World is Nahtazu.

In fact, Nahtazu is so big...

> *All together now... "How big is it, Dad?"*

It's so big that the other 3 parks combined would almost fit inside of it.

> *Really? That's crazy.*

Crazy, but true. Animal Kingdom is around 500 acres. Shoot, Magic Kingdom would fit inside Kilimanjaro Safaris* alone.

> *So what does all of this size stuff have to do with creating MY PLAN for Animal Kingdom?*

So we're back to calling it Animal Kingdom?

> *I never called it anything else. You did.*

Kilimanjaro Safaris is the star attraction of Animal Kingdom - it's a live safari adventure where guests ride in special vehicles through landscapes populated by REAL animals.

Good point. OK, Animal Kingdom it is.

Are you always this easily distracted?

Yep. Squirrel!* (There's a whole herd of them nesting in my office.)

   Focus Dad.

Let's get back to the matter at hand. What was it? I forgot (squirrel).

   A PLAN for Animal Kingdom.

Oh, yeah. That's right. Animal Kingdom Plan. Let's see...

Dad's Simple Fun Magic Guide to YOUR PLAN for Animal Kingdom.

Animal Kingdom is the easiest park to plan for because basically it's laid out in one big oval. It kind of looks like a NASCAR track.

But it's the hardest park when it comes to execution because of all the "Squirrels", and yes, I am talking about distractions.

There are some really cool distractions in Animal Kingdom that can throw off any PLAN. We'll talk more about that in a minute.

So, lets get started!

   It's about time.

Step 1 – The best way to tackle Animal Kingdom is to pick a spot on the oval and work your way around the park. Pick a spot, any spot.

Yes, it's that Simple. Wasn't that Fun? Did you feel the Magic?

   Dad, one step? Really?

*In the 2009 Pixar film, Up, a character named Dug is easily distracted by squirrels (real and imaginary).

What about Dad's Rules, FastPass+, Extra Magic Hours, and all that stuff? Did you forget?

Details, details. Who cares about details?

(Loud foot tapping...)

OK, you win.

Step 2 – Make FastPass+ reservations based on your projected time to be in the vicinity. Get to the park early. Have a Plan. Sound familiar? Yep, Dad's 3 Simple Rules for Conquering the Theme Parks at Walt Disney World.

Is that better?

Step 3 – Execute.

Squirrels

Here's where it gets complicated. Following a PLAN at Animal Kingdom can be hard because of all the Squirrels.

Now do you get it?

Animal Kingdom is all about managing distractions.

Everywhere you turn there is another distraction. Some of these Squirrels can take hours. Check this list out:

- The Oasis Exhibits
- Discovery Island Trails
- Gorilla Falls Exploration Trail
- Rafiki's Planet Watch
- Maharajah Jungle Trek
- Pandora – The World of AVATAR

And those are just the ones listed on the map.

Along those trails, there are lots and lots of animals that just suck you in. You'll spend time looking for them, watching them, and even talking to the Cast Members about them. It's mesmerizing.

You might even go a little Dr. Doolittle…

If I could talk to the animals…

Wouldn't that be cool? Hey Mr. Hippo, how's the water?

It's not that these Squirrels are a bad thing. I'm not saying you should skip them. NOT AT ALL. They are part of what makes Animal Kingdom the most uniquest Theme Park in the world.

What I am saying is you have to manage your time. Build time in YOUR PLAN for these "Squirrels."

Like this:

Rafiki's Planet Watch

A couple of years ago, we went to Walt Disney World with the all growed (yes, I know that's not a word) up kids and their spouses, for the first time.

The Man-Child is a certified animal nut. He could spend weeks in Animal Kingdom just watching the animals. He probably should have been a Veterinarian or something.

One of the things we had never done at Animal Kingdom is go back to Rafiki's Planet Watch. It never made the cut when we made our list of the rides we would go on.

The Man-Child would always rank it high on his list and everyone else would rank it low. Sorry, son.

That all changed. The Man-Child now had help. His wife. She voted it high (actually I think he just filled out her form and never even showed it to her). So off to Rafiki's we went.

I must say, Rafiki's was not what I had expected...

For years, I had read about Rafiki's and the conservation message that it pushed. Rafiki's Planet Watch. Conservation Station. Those are the type of things we typically try to miss at WDW. So we'd always skipped Rafiki's.

After 15 years of skipping Rafiki's, we finally jumped on the train and headed back. THE PLAN allotted 53 minutes. Everyone knew EXACTLY how long we had so there would be no whining when it was time to move on.

(This sounds a little cruel to The Man-Child, but the next thing on the list was Flights of Wonder, which is his favorite show at Walt Disney World, he was OK with THE PLAN.)

We got back to Rafiki's and found it to be really cool. The train ride was Fun. I'm a big train fan. I could ride on a train all day and the train to Rafiki's gives you a different perspective since you ride sideways.

We started walking through Rafiki's and ended up in the Conservation Station, which was not at all like I envisioned it. There were lots of interesting exhibits.

A few minutes after we arrived, Tarzan came out and started interacting with the kids. It was amazing to watch how the little ones looked at him and how he communicated without words. That Tarzan was really great.

The Cast Member on the trail told us that they were bringing a tiger in for a checkup. It was supposed to happen about 20 minutes after we arrived. At the 20-minute mark we heard someone say the arrival had been delayed until 10:25, which was 7 minutes after our scheduled departure time.

I knew The Man-Child was dying to see what they were going to do to the tiger, so I asked him if he wanted to stay, or head to Flights of Wonder? (The rest of the family didn't care. Yes, I asked them too.)

> He chose Flights of Wonder, so off we went. We stayed on schedule. I managed the distraction.

Yep, I was King of the Lab, the Conquering Hero of one of the biggest of distractions and pretty Hot Stuff!

Mmmm, Solo Sport?

That's a really good point Pigment.

What I meant to say is together the family managed the distraction of the tiger having surgery. We avoided the Squirrel and kept OUR PLAN on track.

Was that better?

Much better. Thank you!

You're welcome.

That's it, that's all there is creating YOUR PLAN for Animal Kingdom. Pick a spot and go around the oval and manage the distractions.

Don't forget to do the busy rides first!

SimpleFunMagic.com/The-Busy-Rides

This might help. Yes, it's time for the Rate-A-Ride Spreadsheet. This time for Animal Kingdom.

SimpleFunMagic.com/Rate-A-Ride-AK

Dad's Bottom Line

OK, pay attention here. This is big. The One Big Secret for Animal Kingdom is to manage the distractions. That's it. That's the whole secret to navigating Animal Kingdom. Squirrels.

The Next Step

Now, we have to find out what else there is to see and do at Walt Disney World. Or as I like to call it, (Imagine a big announcer voice with a lot of reverb saying...) *Beyond the Theme Parks...*

Oh, that sounds like Fun!

It will be, Pigment. It will be.

BEYOND THE PARKS
PLANS FOR THE WATER PARKS, DISNEY SPRINGS, AND MORE

"There's a great, big, beautiful tomorrow... Just a dream away!"
- Carousel of Progress*

Speaking of squirrels...

Now that we've got a PLAN for dealing with the Theme Parks, we need take a Magic carpet ride to look at "A Whole New World" outside of the Theme Parks.

SimpleFunMagic.com/A-Whole-New-World

"A Whole New World**" is one of my favorite Disney movie songs ever. That's saying something. Disney has lots of great movie songs.

"A Whole New World"

Outside of the Theme Parks, there is "A Whole New World" to be explored. I think I've mentioned that WDW is over 27,000 acres and the theme parks just cover about 1,000 of them. That leaves a whole lot of room for other "distractions."

---

*Carousel of Progress is an attraction which debuted at the 1964 New York World's Fair before being relocated to Disneyland and finally Magic Kingdom's Tomorrowland. **"A Whole New World" is the love ballad in the 1992 Disney Animated Classic, Aladdin.

And boy does Disney have some incredible distractions! You might Simply say, these distractions are Fun, and truly have some Disney Magic.

Subtle with the Simple, Fun, Magic thing there, Dad. Really subtle.

Did you like that?

Move along, there's nothing to see here. These aren't the robots you're looking for.

Disney even has a special ticket option that covers this "Whole New World." It's called the Park Hopper Plus option.

What is Park Hopper Plus?

If you buy a one-day or multi-day ticket with the Park Hopper option, you can upgrade for a fee to a Park Hopper Plus ticket. This will entitle you to a certain number of "visits" to any of the following non-theme park activities at WDW:

- **Water Parks** – Blizzard Beach and Typhoon Lagoon
- **Mini Golf** – Winter Summerland, Fantasia Gardens
- **9-hole Golf** – Disney's Oak Trail Golf Course
- **ESPN Wide World of Sports Complex**

But there's a lot more Fun around Walt Disney World that you don't need a ticket for.

- **Disney Springs** – Over 150 shops, restaurants and entertainment options.
- **The BoardWalk** – More shops, restaurants and entertainment.
- **Golf Courses** – Disney's Magnolia Golf Course, Disney's Palm Golf Course, and Lake Buena Vista Golf Course.
- **Sports** - Tennis, Basketball, Running Trails, Exercise Facilities, Fishing, Boating, Parasailing, Swimming, Biking, Horseback Riding, Surfing, etc.
- **Spa Treatments**

That's quite a list Dad, how are we going to see and do all of it?

The good news is, you don't have to. There's a lot of it that I have never, and probably will never do. Running tracks - not for Dad.

What's important to YOU?

As you create YOUR PLAN, you need to decide What's important to YOU. If it's spring, summertime or fall, you might want to visit the Water Parks. The water parks are open almost every day.

You might be one of those crazy runner types, who need to run every day.

For all I know, you might think that spending a day in Disney Springs is more important that spending a day at Disney's Hollywood Studios. That's totally up to YOU. You might be a spa person and want to have a spa day. That's totally what YOU should do.

Remember this is YOUR PLAN. What is important to YOU?

Is there a mud bath somewhere?

I don't know about that one Pigment.

Let's talk about the different options in what I'm calling Water Park Fun and More.

Water parks

When we talk about Water Park Fun and More, we probably should start with talking about the Water Parks.

Walt Disney World has two of the best Water Parks anywhere. I'm a little biased, but I don't know where you'll find more Fun at a Water Park.

It's kind of hard to call the Disney Water Parks "distractions." They are more like water-based theme parks.

Making a PLAN for the Water Parks is almost as important as the theme parks.

You'll be surprised at how busy they get during the day.

So let's talk about a Water Park Plan. It's actually pretty Simple.

Dad's Simple Fun Magic Guide to YOUR PLAN for the Water Parks at WDW

(Whew. That title is getting longer all the time.)

Step 1 – Follow Dad's 3 Simple Rules for Conquering the Theme Parks at Walt Disney World to get on all the slides and raft rides you want to.

Step 2 – Spend the rest of the day in the "Lazy River," bobbing around in the wave pool, or enjoying the sandy beaches.

Step 3 – Execute.

It's pretty Simple to PLAN for the Water Parks. Both Blizzard Beach and Typhoon Lagoon follow the same patterns as the Theme Parks.

If you follow Dad's Simple Rules… get to the park early, have a plan and ride the busy rides first you'll have a great day. (Yes, there is another Rule but the Water Parks don't have FastPass+.)

SimpleFunMagic.com/Rate-A-Ride-Water-Parks

Disney Springs

The second big "distraction" on Dad's Water Park Fun and More list is Disney Springs.

With the expansion of Disney Springs, it's almost like Walt Disney World now has 5 theme parks. There is so much to see and do, you could spend a full day at Disney Springs and still not experience everything.

Disney says that Disney Springs is a "charming waterside dining, shopping and entertainment destination." That sounds so innocent…

Oh, I've got to run over and spend an hour or two looking at this charming little location…

That was true several years ago but now...

Disney Springs is a monster. It's huge. It's a mile-long dining, shopping, and entertainment destination. There are now over 150 shops, restaurants, and entertainment options.

I could probably write a whole book on Disney Springs alone. There's as much to do and see in Disney Springs as in the Magic Kingdom.

See more about Disney Springs over on the website...

SimpleFunMagic.com/Disney-Springs

Disney Springs has some of the best restaurants at Walt Disney World. And that's saying something.

> *So Dad, what's the PLAN for Disney Springs? How do we get to be the HOT, lab conquering, king of stuff or whatever it was?*

A Disney Springs PLAN is pretty easy. Get off the bus and just start wandering around. When you come to a fork in the road, take it.

Boom. Done.

I'm not kidding. It's pretty Simple. There's really only one path (with a couple of short detours), and it runs the whole length of Disney Springs. Walk down that path to the end then turn around and go the other way.

Yes we even have a Rate-A-Thing Spreadsheet for Disney Springs.

SimpleFunMagic.com/Rate-A-Thing

Disney's BoardWalk

The other shopping, dining, and entertainment complex at WDW is Disney's BoardWalk. The BoardWalk is home to Disney's version of "adult" entertainment.

The BoardWalk area is tied to Disney's BoardWalk Inn and Villas Resort. It's located just behind Epcot, you can actually walk out of the back of Epcot (at the International Gateway) and be on the BoardWalk in just a couple of minutes.

The BoardWalk is modeled after a 1930's Atlantic City seaside village. It's a quaint area of shops, restaurants, entertainment, and, as Dad calls them, "adult beverage establishments."

If you have a few hours some evening, take a stroll on the BoardWalk. You might even find yourself taking a surrey bike on a sunset ride. That would be kind of cool.

See more here...

 SimpleFunMagic.com/The-BoardWalk

There's not much really to PLAN for when it comes to the BoardWalk. It's just a time management thing. Most of the Fun and games on the BoardWalk happen in the evenings.

Take an hour (or two) when you are at Epcot and stroll the BoardWalk – or not. If you are so inclined, you can stop into one of the "adult beverage establishments," and grab a drink, or two.

All of the rest

Yes, I'm going to lump all of the rest of the Water Park Fun and More lists together, when it comes to planning. There are a couple of reasons. First, I don't have a lot of experience with most of them. Other than golf, I don't do sports (and certainly not on vacation) and I'm not a spa kind of guy.

Basically, you know how long it takes if you are into those kinds of things. Build that time into YOUR REAL PLAN. Simple. Fun. Magic. Drop the mic.

You can't see it all

One of the most important things I can tell you about a trip to Walt Disney World is that you can't see it all. I know, I've said this already, but I think that it's important to repeat here.

You will not be able to do everything at Walt Disney World. Trust me. I've been over 20 times and I still haven't.

If you can't do it at home...

One of our main goals when we go to WDW is to do the things that we can't do at home. Me, I love playing golf. I could probably play a round of golf just about every day of our vacation and be very happy.

But, I can do that at home. Yes, the Disney golf courses are nice, but they aren't that different from what I can do here in beautiful Oklahoma. So, I don't play golf at Walt Disney World (OK, I did one time but that was back when there were just 2 parks and we didn't have kids with us).

For the most part, when we go to Walt Disney World we try to do the things we just can't find at home. Why go to a movie at Disney Springs? I can do that at home. I can't ride Space Mountain at home.

If, and only IFF

So our rule of thumb is to put the things we can't do at home high on the priority list. The rest, we do IFF we have time.

(Yes, I meant to say IFF. Back in my computer programmer days one of the logical expressions (computer term) I learned was IFF. IFF stood for, if and only if. I've forgotten exactly what it was used for, but it seems to fit what we're talking about here.)

The Water Park Fun and More options are there for you, IFF they fit into YOUR PLAN.

Dad's Bottom Line

Water Park Fun and More is all about YOU.
What do YOU like? What do YOU want to do?
That's great. Write it down. Put it in YOUR PLAN.

Yes, it's that Simple. It's about YOU having Fun.
That's what makes the Magic!

The Next Step

Someone said I need to talk a little more about shopping. Did you know there are places to shop at Walt Disney World? Lots of them.

Can I go shopping at Disney World Dad?

Maybe, Pigment. Maybe.

15

'TILL YOU DROP
SHOPPING AND SOUVENIERS

"Ah, buenos dias, senorita.
My siestas are getting chorter and chorter."
- The Enchanted Tiki Room*

OK, so we're done with the overview of the parks and beyond, so now it's time to move on to the final details of YOUR PLAN.

Uh, Dad.

Yes, Pigment. What now?

I think you're forgetting something.
Something very important.

And what would that be?

Uh…. Shopping?!?!

Shopping? I don't do any shopping. Mrs. Mom
usually takes care of that. Why would I possibly want to talk about shopping?

The Enchanted Tiki Room is a musical show in Adventureland at Magic Kingdom. which features Audio-Animatronic birds.

Oh, oh. OH! OH MY GOODNESS! How on earth did I forget that? Yes, yes, we need to talk about shopping at WDW!

Pigment is right. We definitely need to talk about What you will shop for at Walt Disney World.

The silly hat

"You want what? Son, that hat is just silly. Tigger? I didn't think you liked Tigger. It's going to take all your money. This is just the first day. What if you see something tomorrow you want more? Then what are you going to do?"

Yes, I was trying hard to talk The Man-Child out of it. Mrs. Mom was too. "No, you don't need a silly Christmas Tigger Stocking Cap." It was the silliest looking thing ever.

"But it's cold outside and I need something to cover my ears. This is perfect!"

But the boy was set. The more Mrs. Mom and I said no, the more he dug in. (That happened a lot with The Man-Child.) His grandmother had given him money so he had the money to buy it himself. He did.

Turns out it worked out pretty well. He wore that hat for years.

SimpleFunMagic.com/Follow-That-Tigger

You WILL shop at WDW

I don't care who you are, even a big, dopey, 15-year old kid, you will shop at WDW. Yes, you will. Trust me.

How do I know you that will shop at WDW? Because, Disney is the absolute best at creating merchandise that you will want to buy and then putting it right where you want to buy it the most.

For example, you ride Star Tours: The Adventures Continue and you're just a little uneasy coming out of the simulator, so where is the exit? Right over there, after you go through Tatooine Traders gift shop. Oh did you see where you can build your own Lightsaber? That's so cool!

I want to build a Lightsaber, Dad! Can I, can I?

No Pigment. We'll be in a hurry. You won't have time.

How do you know that?

We're always in a hurry. Come on. We've got to keep moving.

You're mean!

It's not just the gift shops after the rides, it's...

- The shops on Main Street USA
- The biggest Disney Store in the world at Disney Springs
- The Pin Trading kiosks located all throughout the parks
- The glow gear carts that pop up at the nighttime shows
- All the stores in the World Showcase where you can get "stuff" from around the world
- The cool gift shops in the hotels
- The limited time souvenir cups and t-shirts

...and, the list goes on and on.

Everyone spends at least a little time in a gift shop. You can't help it. You WILL shop at Walt Disney World (and you will like it).

This isn't one of those Jedi* mind trick things you're trying to pull is it?

Mmm, I never quite thought of it that way. It sure seems like it might be, because shopping at WDW is so addicting...

(Shaking head) No, it can't be. Disney and shopping started long before George Lucas dreamed up Star Wars.

*The Jedi are the good guys in the Star Wars franchise, and one of their powers is mind control.

Good try though Pigment.

Thank you!

At some point everyone does some
major shopping at Walt Disney World. Which
can be a problem if you aren't prepared.

*So now I suppose you are going to tell us
how to prepare?*

That's kind of the point of the whole book, isn't it?
Let's dive right in.

The budget

One of the very first things we talked about in *Dad's Simple Fun Magic Guide to Walt Disney World Planning* was the need to make a budget. It was way back in the intro. The "B" Word.

Remember the "little" help? Remember the trip budget spreadsheet you created? Did you fill in the line for Shopping? Good job!

So, now you have a shopping budget. A shopping budget is a handy thing to have. It limits how much you can spend on all the cool stuff that miraculously seems to end up in your room at the end of the trip.

The Princess was the first grandchild on Mrs. Mom's side of the family. When Mrs. Mom's Mom used to go to the mall things would just jump in her basket for the grandkids.

That's what happens at Walt Disney World. Things just jump in the basket and before you know it's you've spent a bazillion dollars on things you can't fit in your suitcase.

That's why you need a shopping budget. Even for the kids.

We've always controlled what the kids could spend by giving them Disney Dollars (sadly, you can't get Disney Dollars any more, but you could use cold hard cash or a Disney gift card!). We gave them a set amount and that was their spending money for the trip.

And yes, we even gave them Disney Dollars on the "grown up" trip. It was a Fun tradition.

Giving the kids money to spend and not letting them spend more than they have is a good way to teach them the value of money and the importance of budgeting it.

You have to get it home

One of the big things to think about when you are shopping at Walt Disney World is: how are you going to get that thing home?

> *What do you mean by that Dad? They can just throw it in the suitcase. What's the big deal?*

That's fine Pigment, if you have a big enough suitcase. In fact, I have friends that actually take an extra suitcase just for the things they plan to buy at Walt Disney World.

Leaving room in the suitcase is something you have to plan for. To be prepared for.

Oh, and those cute balloons they sell are hard to get home. Just saying.

> *I love those cute balloons. Can I have one?*

Probably not, Pigment. Probably not.

> *Oh, Dad, I've got a great idea. I won't buy anything at Walt Disney World, I'll just wait and buy it online when I get home.*

Not everything is available online

My friend Kristi just got back from Walt Disney World last week (OK, it was last week as I'm writing this, but probably months or even years ago as you read it).

She told me about her shopping experience at WDW and it triggered this whole chapter.

> *So now the real story comes out about "the forgotten chapter."*

Yes, but that's a whole different story. Let me stay on track.

You got it, boss.

(Leave it alone, Dad. Leave it alone.)

Kristi said she was walking through the Magic Kingdom on the first day of her trip. She found something she wanted to buy early in the morning but decided she'd come back later in the day and get it.

At the end of the day, guess what? She didn't want to traipse back to that gift shop and buy it. The family was tired so she didn't get it. She decided she'd get it later or at home online. Everything's available online. Right?

NOT!!!

When she got home and checked out the Disney Store website, guess what?

It wasn't there, was it?

That's right, Pigment. It wasn't there.

The Disney Store Online has recently started carrying some park merchandise, but not a lot. Chances are really good that you won't be able to get that cool Tigger Christmas Stocking Hat online, or much of anything else you see at the parks.

Kristi, like many others, was out of luck.

That's it? She was out of luck? What kind of friend are you? Did you tell her where she could find it or something?

No, but I did remind her that she could have gone ahead and purchased the item and had it sent to her room from the gift shop or picked it up at the front gate when she left for the day.

She was very happy when I reminded her about that.

I'm so helpful.

> *Yeah, helpful… Maybe you should share how that sent to the room and front gate things works.*

Yes, I should. But we'll throw that over on the website.

SimpleFunMagic.com/Package-Delivery

Dad's Bottom Line

YOU will shop while you are at Walt Disney World. You will! Make a budget before you go. Think about how you are going to get things home. Don't miss out on a great souvenir thinking you can buy it later.

Those are the basics of shopping at Walt Disney World.

The Next Step

It's time to take a little break from all this planning and have some Fun. Let's play a game.

> *I like playing games, Dad.*

Me too, Pigment. Me too.

"Think of all the joy you'll find, when you leave the world behind and bid your cares goodbye! You can fly, you can fly, you can fly!"
- Peter Pan's Flight*

Time for recess.

Oh boy, I like recess. It was my favorite part of school.

I'm sure it was, Pigment. I'm sure it was...

After all that "school work" it's probably time to take a break and have some Fun! Take it away Barry...

Barry and friends are right. You deserve a break today (bet you didn't know Barry wrote THAT).

You've been working hard. I'm sure you're a little stressed about the trip.

*Peter Pan's Flight is a dark ride attraction in Fantasyland at Magic kingdom, based on the 1953 Disney Animated Classic, Peter Pan.

I'm sure you're a little stressed about whether or not this Dad guy is ever going to get through this planning thing. Hey, life is stressful.

PAAAARTAHY time!

I've got just the thing. I think it's time to have a little, or maybe a big, PAAAARTAHY!!!!! (That's PARTY for you that don't speak Dad.)

> Hey Dad, hmmmmm, what's going on? I've never heard of a book taking a break in the middle for a party.

To paraphrase what Robin Williams* said, you ain't never read a book like this.

> That's for sure. But Dad...

This book is different. It's Fun. Have you ever seen another Disney book like this one?

> Nope, and I'm...

Stop it, Pigment, before you say something I don't want to hear.

Time to have some Fun!

I think it's vital to the success of any trip to have a little laughter, to have Fun. One of the main goals of this book is to add Fun to YOUR Disney World vacation.

And I meant it when I said you deserve it.

Not only do you deserve a break, your whole family deserves a break from the everyday stresses and strains of normal life. Let's see if we can't make that happen.

Laughter is the best medicine

Mrs. Mom likes to read in bed and every month when the *Reader's Digest*

---

*The Genie was played by Robin Williams in the 1992 Disney Animated Classic, Aladdin.

comes she reads it to me. No, not all of it, but usually the section called "Laughter is the Best Medicine."

There's normally a Funny story, or 4, she shares. It's a Simple little time of Fun. Don't tell her, but I really enjoy it when she shares those stories. Yes, I could read them myself, but there's some Magic when they come from her.

It's been scientifically proven that laughter is good for you. So, let me don my best Mike Wazowski* suit (yes, one eye and all) and see if I can't brighten up your day, and help you share a little Fun with the family as you plan YOUR trip.

Shall we play a game?

I grew up in the 70's (no, it wasn't like *That's 70's Show* at our house, but I did have a tall redhead for a girlfriend come to think of it).

What does that have to do with Fun?

I don't know, but somehow it slipped in.

One of the blockbuster movies during the 70's was *War Games*. What a cool movie.

I love the scene when Matthew Broderick first talks to "Joshua" (the computer) and Joshua says, in the best computer voice ever, "shall we play a game?"

Oh, yes! I love playing games. I'm really good at it and I cheat.

Anyone else not surprised that Dad cheats?

That hurts.

Moving on, let's get started…

Mike Wazowski is a character from the Disney/Pixar films Monsters Inc. and Monster's University, and is the "monster of ceremonies" at Monsters Inc. Laugh Floor in the Magic Kingdom.

YouTube scavenger hunt

How about a YouTube Scavenger Hunt? Doesn't that sound like Fun?

Here you go. We've put together a long list of Fun things to find on a Walt Disney World YouTube Video Scavenger Hunt.

Family Fun time

One of the things I think really makes a Walt Disney World vacation even more Magical is building anticipation (no I'm not going to play the ketchup song).

Who am I kidding...

I love Carly.

Disney makes it really easy to build anticipation.

One of the ways to build anticipation by using a series of Family Fun Nights. We even have some suggestions to how to build them into your planning schedule.

Since schedules change all the time, we decided to create a few pages with suggestions of Family Fun Activities.

Some of the activities we have include:

Disney family movie nights

One of the Simplest ways to build anticipation is through Disney Family Movie Nights.

This is so Simple. There are about a hundred Disney movies out on VHS/ Beta etc.

Dad, really VHS and Beta? For goodness sake how old are you?

Just trying to see if you were still paying attention.

Whatever method you choose to watch movies on, you can find all the Disney movies.

In fact, just about every Friday night on Freeform (what used to be ABC Family), Disney runs one of their blockbuster movies.

Yes, I know, you don't have cable anymore. Watch a DVD. A Blu-ray. Even Netflix!

Try to make Disney Family Movie Night a special treat. Make some popcorn, character themed treats, or even Dole Whips (we'll talk about how to do that in a minute), and celebrate your trip with the movie. You can talk with the kids about which characters they want to see when they get to WDW and the rides that have characters in them.

SimpleFunMagic.com/Family-Movie-Night

Disney game night

Pull the Disney Games out of the drawer and have some Fun. Or go online to the Disney Store and get a few new ones. You'll find the link at:

SimpleFunMagic.com/Family-Game-Night

There is nothing that brings a family together more than putting down the phones and playing games together.

Walt Disney World recipes

"Do you want to make a Dole Whip?" (Sung to the tune of "Do You Want to Build a Snowman?"*)

"Do You Want to Build a Snowman?" is a song from the 2013 Disney Animated Classic, Frozen.

Come on, Dad, not everything needs to be sung like Frozen…

You're right, Pigment, but it's Fun, and frozen (little f) treats get a pass.

A great way to build anticipation is by cooking and sharing some of your favorite Disney foods. The recipes for almost every popular food served at Walt Disney World are available online.

Go find one and give it a try. There are Mickey Waffles, Dole Whips, 'Ohana Bread Pudding, and even the Peanut Butter and Jelly Shake from 50's Prime Time Café.

Got a bit of a sweet tooth there, Dad?

Mmmmm, might be. Do you wonder what Dad likes to eat at Walt Disney World?

Like I said, you can pretty much find all the favorite (and some pretty obscure) recipes online. Have some Fun with them and build some anticipation.

We have some recipes all ready for you to try at…

☑ SimpleFunMagic.com/Family-Recipes

Children's games, crafts puzzles and coloring pages

A few years ago, I started *WDW Magazine*. One of the first things I wanted to add was a way to bring the Magic of Walt Disney World to your Home.

In fact, we had a section called Bring The Magic Home, where we would have crafts, games, and things you could do with the kids to really bring the feeling of Walt Disney World right to your living room.

We expanded Bring the Magic Home to a whole section for kids we call Section k! In Section k! we have Bring the Magic Home along with word puzzles, coloring pages and cartoons, recipes, children's stories, and more!

We've pulled out some of our favorites and added them to the Family Fun Night page.

☑ SimpleFunMagic.com/Family-Activites

Shoot, while we're having Fun, how about another commercial? Those are Fun.

Wasn't that whole section just a big commercial for WDW Magazine Dad?

It does kind of feel that way, doesn't it? OK, no full blown commercial, but BUY WDW Magazine today!

❗ SimpleFunMagic.com/WDW-Magazine

Dad's Bottom Line

Now wasn't that a nice break? You deserve a break every once in a while. It recharges the batteries and gets you ready for what's coming next.

NO, I'm not saying it's going to get worse, I'm just saying now that we're all recessed, refreshed and ready, let's move on.

The Next Step

Now that the schooling is all over, it's time to make a little Magic.

🎵 SimpleFunMagic.com/Make-A-Little-Magic

Magic. Ooooooh, Magic is Fun. I like Magic.

Me too, Pigment. Me too.

MAGIC

"PLUSSING" YOUR VACATION

It seems like every Disney movie ever made has some connection with "Magic." All the classics – Snow White, Cinderella, Pinocchio, Fantasia, and more – center around Magic. Shoot, even The Love Bug has a talking car.

But it's not just the classics, look at the more recent movies, *Aladdin, The Little Mermaid, Beauty and the Beast,* and yes, even the Pixar movies where cars, dinosaurs and toys come alive.

You're going to Walt Disney World. Your vacation needs a little Magic!

That's what we are going to do. I'm going to conjure up a little Magic and we'll finish this off.

SimpleFunMagic.com/Its-Magic

It's Magic, you know… Never believe it's not so…

So Dad, how are you going to do this "Magic" thing? Are you going to turn blue and, sing "Bibbidi, Bobbidi, Boo*" or something? Are you going to fly around and have Pixie Dust come out? Are you going to grab a Magic baton and go all Sorcerer's Apprentice** on us?

---

*"Bibbidi, Bobbidi, Boo" is a song from the 1950 Disney Animated Classic, Cinderella.
**The Sorcerer's Apprentice is a vignette from the 1940 Disney Animated Classic, Fantasia.

Not exactly Pigment.

We started off the book with Scar telling us we need to be prepared for the trip of a lifetime (rough paraphrase). That's where the Magic is. It's in the preparation.

So Dad, once again I ask, how are you going to do this Magic thing? Do we need to rub a lamp? Do you have a Magical trident? Is there a red rose or glass slipper somewhere that will make all our dreams come true?

No, Pigment, nothing like that. I'm going to talk about some final details that will help you "be prepared" for the trip of a lifetime. The final details that separate "the men from the boys" that truly will make a trip Magic.

This section is going to cover how to "Plus*" your vacation.

I've got to see this.

OK, so here's what we're going to cover in Section Magic…

- Getting ready for your trip
- What to do when Stuff Happens – and it will
- Being ready for anything and everything
- The Final Exam – it's time to put it all together
- Packing
- When it's time to go!
- The cure for ADVBS

Dad's Bottom Line

The Magic in a Disney vacation really is all about preparation and in this section I am going to get you prepared!

Walt Disney was famous for telling his team to "Plus It" when something was good, but needed a little extra oomph to make it really special.

The Next Step

It's time to talk about the most important chapter in this whole book. It's time to talk about how to get ready for your Walt Disney World vacation.

Dad, I was BORN ready!

Me too, Pigment. Me too.

THE MOST IMPORTANT CHAPTER
GETTING READY

"Come on Baby, let's do the Twist."
– Pop Century*, 8am "exercise class"

"The Most Important Chapter?" What on earth could be more important than having a good PLAN? Dad, haven't you been pounding the point home that everyone needs a PLAN for a Walt Disney World vacation? And now, after we write our PLAN you say something else is more important?

Have you gone totally crazy?

No, Pigment, I haven't gone totally crazy. Trust me on this one.

OK, you're the boss.

Let's get this started with a little question.

What is the MOST IMPORTANT thing you should take on a Walt Disney World vacation?

*At Disney's Pop Century Resort, guests can join along with Cast Members every morning at 8am in Classic Hall and learn to do The Twist. Or, at 6pm each night, try out The Hustle. Groovy.

That's easy. Sunscreen. Have you seen what a sunburned pig looks like? It's not pretty.

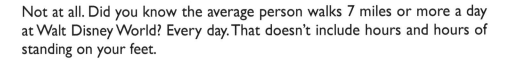

That's a good one, but there's something more important.

We could play this game all day. Why don't we save some time and you just tell us the answer?

OK. That's fair. The MOST IMPORTANT thing you should take on the trip of a lifetime is comfortable, well broken-in shoes.

Shoes? You've got to be kidding.

Not at all. Did you know the average person walks 7 miles or more a day at Walt Disney World? Every day. That doesn't include hours and hours of standing on your feet.

By the end of a day, your feet will be tired, very tired and very sore even if you have good shoes.

And if you don't have the MOST IMPORTANT thing, you might be starring in...

Not only will Fear* be freaking out but so will your feet!

That would be sad.

I can't believe I'm about to ask this question. Are there any shoes you recommend?

Me, I wear sneakers because that's what I wear every day and I'm the most

---

"The Shoes of Doom" is a fictional movie mentioned in a promotional featurette for Disney/ Pixar's Inside Out. Fear is a character in Inside Out.

comfortable in, but everyone has to choose what's most comfortable for them.

But everyone has to pick the shoes they are most comfortable in.

> **Socks Too:** Not only is it important to have good comfortable shoes, but socks too. While shoes might make the man, socks are what keep the shoes comfy.

Time to get in shape

Oh, oh, oh… Speaking of important things, one of the best things you can do for your feet as you prepare for your WDW vacation is to get in shape.

Get in shape. You are going to talk about getting in shape? I am literally rolling on the floor laughing. ROFL. Ha. Ha. Ha. You are a Funny man.

Don't laugh. I'm serious.

A WDW vacation is murder on the body if you're not prepared.

OK, Dad. We get it. We need to do a little to get our bodies ready for our trip. Are YOU going to tell us how?

Dad the exercise guru – Funny!

Yes, I'm just about the last guy in the whole world to give exercise advice. When it comes to exercise, you'd think that I was allergic to it. I'm one of those guys whose bodies went from being jock like to Pooh-like after high school.

Yes, I meant to say Pooh-like. I went from looking like Michael Phelps (in my dreams) to looking like Winnie the Pooh.

SimpleFunMagic.com/Pooh-Excercise

Dad's about as much of an exercise guru as Winnie the Pooh, but there is one thing I do know: when it comes to Walt Disney World vacations, it's very important to get your body prepared for the pounding it's going to take. So, let's talk about a few things you can do to start getting ready in the weeks and months before your trip.

Dad's radical, new "Get My Body Ready For WDW" plan

There is no real way to simulate just what you will be facing when you get to Walt Disney World. But I have my (patent pending) brand new, radical plan to help you get ready for WDW. I call it my "Get My Body Ready for WDW Plan." Check it out at:

SimpleFunMagic.com/Dads-Radical-New-Plan

Want to make a life change? Do you need some encouragement?

Encouragement is always good. We've started a group of fellow SFM'ers who are trying to make a life change. I'm a big part of the group and I hope you'll join us as we look to get in shape for not only Walt Disney World vacations, but for a better life.

Get all the details:

SimpleFunMagic.com/The-Excercise-Group

Dad's Bottom Line

Yes! This chapter is the MOST IMPORTANT chapter in the whole book. The most important thing you can do to get ready for your vacation is to get in shape. I'm serious. This is important. Not only for Walt Disney World, but for life. YOUR LIFE!

Get up. Put on some comfy shoes! Get on your feet. Eat better. Eat less. It's Simple. You can make it Fun. The results will be nothing short of Magic!

Come on. You'll thank me!

The Next Step

We're going to talk about what to do when things don't go exactly right.

I don't like it when things don't go right.

Me either, Pigment. Me either.

STUFF HAPPENS
WHEN THINGS GO WRONG

"And don't worry about that asteroid; you'll be in and out
of there before it even breaks the atmosphere.
Trust me, what could go wrong?"
- DINOSAUR*

Welcome to the Spookiest, the Scariest, the most Stressful chapter in this book.

Dun-dun-duuuuuunnnnn.

Relax. Dad is on the job. You ain't never had a friend like Dad.

SimpleFunMagic.com/Never-Had-a-Friend

This is going to be good!

Stuff happens

Stuff Happens. That phrase is so descriptive. It's so apt. It's hard to argue with. Even at the Most Magical Place on Earth, Stuff Happens.

*DINOSAUR is a time travel themed thrill ride in DinoLand U.S.A. at Animal Kingdom.

Stuff like:

- Forgetting to set the alarm and realizing you're late
- A ride breaks down
- Little Johnny isn't tall enough to ride.
- Someone gets sick or hurt
- Disney lost our ADRs
- I didn't make ADRs
- Picky eaters
- I need a bathroom NOW
- Someone stole the stroller
- It's RAINING?!?!?
- Cranky kids (…and husbands and wives)
- Forgot the camera
- Promised the kids breakfast with princesses but forgot to make ADRs
- It's too hot
- There's a problem at home
- Disney changed the schedule
- The kids are bored
- It's HOW LONG to meet Elsa?!?!
- We missed our FastPass+
- Pushy people at parades
- Staying awake for the fireworks
- Spills
- Allergies
- The losing battle against souvenir shops
- Characters are too scary for the little one
- Kids just want to swim
- Didn't get the room that we'd requested
- The kids are afraid of the dark
- Grouchy guests who dampen your day
- Hubby NEEDS to watch the game
- Not enough DDP credits
- Too many DDP credits
- Blisters!!!!!!!!!!!!!
- Billy goes missing
- End-of-the-day-tired kids (and adults)
- Can't find the rental car.=

Dad, STOP!!!!
Please! You're stressing me out.

Stop? You're telling me to stop in the middle of my book. Sorry, but it doesn't work that way. Stuff Happens! Saying STOP won't make it so.

It's stressful

But you did bring up a really good point, when Stuff Happens, it's stressful. Or should I say StREsSfuL, spooky, scary…

I thought we probably should talk for a minute about how to handle when Stuff Happens. When it's StREsSfuL, when the pressure builds, when things don't go right, when the Magic takes a break.

How do you handle…

I kind of feel like Billy Joel right now Dad. I'm a little spooked, a little StREsSeD out. I need help. Do you know anyone who can help me? Do you have a lamp I could rub?

Wow, I need to work on my introductions. No, Dad's here to help.

I can help. Really I can.

> *But Dad, what do you know about pressure, about stress, about scary things? You live a perfect life.*

(I thought about using the 15-minute laughing baby video. Perfect Life. That's so Funny.)

Dad knows stress

I do know a thing, or two, about pressure, about overwhelm, about StREsS, about being scared.

> *Oh, yeah. You were one of those Air Traffic Controller guys. Right? I hear that's pretty stressful.*

Yes it was. I guess. People say it's one of the most stressful jobs on the planet. But I survived. I don't drink, I don't smoke, I'm still married to the same Mrs. Mom for close to 40 years, and I still have an almost full head of hair - that's not gray.

That being said, I guess it was pretty stressful. When I retired, my blood pressure went down 20 points.

So yes, I'm kind of familiar with Stuff Happening.

I've even had to deal with Stuff Happening at Walt Disney World. Remember the story I told about when I planned a WDW vacation for the first time? Talk about spooky and scary. I may have glossed over how StREsSfuL that really was.

The secret for dealing with stress

Along the way I learned how to deal with Stuff Happening, with pressure, with StREsS and with overwhelm. I learned a big secret.

Here we go, more secrets.

This one is pretty cool. It really is the secret to dealing with pressure, with overwhelm, with StREsS, with Stuff Happening? It's a really good secret. You might say, it's a very Disneyish secret.

Uh, how can I say this nicely? Do you really know a secret for dealing with stress, or is this just another one of your cockamamie...

I thought you were going to be nice...

Would you like it better if I said, one of your crazy secrets?

Nah, I think it would be in my best interest to just ignore this and move on.

Good idea.

The secret to dealing with pressure, with overwhelm, with StREsS, with scary Stuff Happening is...

(No, it doesn't involve rubbing a lamp and hoping for a genie.)

Drum roll please…

Sure miss those guys.

Ok, here's the secret to dealing with pressure, with overwhelm, with StREsS, with Stuff Happening and even with spooky stuff –

This secret is Simple. It's Fun and, as you're about to see, it's Magic!

Come on, sing along with Elsa*…

Now aren't you impressed at the way I worked in a gratuitous Frozen reference?

> *Eye rolling emoji.*

You think I'm kidding? Not at all. When you have pressure, overwhelm, StREsS, the way to deal with it is just start singing with Elsa and Let It Go.

Let it go

Think about this…

Let's say you have a FastPass+ for Splash Mountain. It's your last day at Walt Disney World. You've been waiting all week to ride it. It's your favorite ride. You get to the entrance and they tell you it's broken and don't expect it to be back up today.

What do you do?

*Elsa is one of the main characters from the hit 2013 Disney Animated Classic, Frozen.

Hey, I'd get mad too. I'd probably think some very un-Disney like things in my head. I might even start to lash out at the poor Cast Member who has the terrible job of standing there and smiling when people start going all Darth Vader on them.

But instead I... come on... you know what's coming. All together now...

"Let It Go, let it go..."

The idea of "Let It Go" is not to make things worse. It's the first step to dealing with Stuff Happening. You start by taking a deep breath and relaxing, then you move on to step two.

Deal with it

Step two is to Deal With It.

When a ride breaks down, Deal With It. Getting mad, sulking, crying (come on, you're an adult now), stomping your feet, cursing... None of that is going to make the ride start working.

Take a deep breath, sing a Disney song, or two and move on. Yes, it's sad. But it's not worth ruining the trip over. Stuff Happens.

That's pretty much true of anything on the list, or anything that can happen at WDW. When Stuff Happens... first relax, then take a deep breath, sing "Let It Go," and Deal With It.

Kids get tired. Go take a nap. Hubby gets cranky, give him a churro. Disney messes something up, "Let It Go" and move on.

That doesn't mean you don't tell someone that you are upset or that something is wrong, but it does mean that you Deal With It and move on.

Don't make the situation worse by blowing it up into something bigger than it really is.

Dad's Bottom Line

Stuff Happens and it can be spooky, it can be scary,

it can sure be stressful at the most inopportune times, but you can handle it.

Let It Go, deal with it, and all will be fine.

You have to remember, the One Big Thing…

YOU ARE AT WALT DISNEY WORLD!!!

Don't let something small take away the Magic! Just…

Isn't that Simple? Focus on the Fun, and before you know it, the Magic will be flowing again.

Told you. You ain't never had a friend like me.

The Next Step

We're going to talk a little more on this topic. It's the What To Do In Case Of… chapter.

> *In case of what, Dad?*

Turn the page and find out, Pigment. Turn the page and find out.

IN CASE OF...
BEING READY FOR ANYTHING

"I am Princess Leia of Alderaan. We've placed a rebel spy
vital to the survival of the rebellion in your StarSpeeder.
You must see him/her safely delivered to the coordinates
I'm transmitting to your R2 unit. This is our most desperate hour.
Help me, Star Tours, you're my only hope."
-Star Tours: The Adventures Continue*

Mrs. Mom's Magical Fanny Pack

Mrs. Mom is probably one of the most prepared travelers ever. Her "trip bible" is the most organized and complete travel tool ever invented.

And then there's Mrs. Mom's Magical Fanny Pack. It's truly amazing. It has everything. If I didn't know better, I'd think it was packed by Mary Poppins herself.

SimpleFunMagic.com/Magical-Carpetbag

Every time I need something - Tylenol, tickets, money, Band-Aids – anything, it comes right out of Mrs. Mom's Magical Fanny Pack. It's Magic!

At least almost every time…

*Star Tours: The Adventures Continue is a motion simulator attraction at Disney's Hollywood Studios.

I was in a hurry to get to the Food and Wine Festival**. I had heard about a steak in the Canada Pavilion and I just had to get one (or three).

We had just arrived in Orlando. It was the first day, we were a little behind schedule. We'd been traveling all day and I was hungry.

We threw the luggage on the bed and I was ready to go. Mrs. Mom said, hang on a minute and let me find the Fanny Pack. There she goes again, being practical. I'm hungry and she wants to find the Fanny Pack. Typical.

I paced around the room like a caged lion. I was ready to pounce. "How long will this take?" I said inside my head, but she knew I was impatient and said, "I need to find all the stuff that goes in the Fanny Pack."

Finally Mrs. Mom got tired of my pacing and said, "I don't have everything but I think I have enough. Do you have the ponchos in the backpack?"

"Nah, it's not going to rain, we won't need them," I said very arrogantly. I was hungry. I was ready to go. I was at DISNEY WORLD for goodness sake. It's time to get to the parks. I need my WDW fix. Foot tap, tap, tap, tap, tap…

So off we went. We jumped in the car and headed at the posted speed limit over to Epcot.

Posted speed limit? Really? You?

OK, I sped. What are you a cop and going to write me a ticket? I didn't go that fast. Just a couple of miles an hour over.

Dad, you're straying off the subject again. Oh, and I'm trying to figure out where this is going.

**The Epcot International Food & Wine Festival is a special event held each fall at WDW.*

You're the one that started the speeding thing.

Good point. Proceed.

Thank you.

As we got to Epcot the very first thing that happened is it started to sprinkle. Right as we got out of the car. Yes, Dear, I left the ponchos in the suitcase. Yes, I was in a hurry. We'll just buy some new ones.

So we grabbed some ponchos, put them on, and headed back toward Canada. I was on a mission and that mission was all about STEAK!

(It only rained for 10 minutes, but we had some new ponchos. I think it was the only time it rained on the whole trip. Yes, I was in a little bit of trouble.)

About that time it hit me. I had a headache. My brain hurt. Hey when you have a brain like mine sometimes it gets overworked and needs something to take the edge off.

So I innocently asked Mrs. Mom the most innocuous question ever, "Do you have any Tylenol?" I've asked it a thousand times. It's always answered the same way. Not this time.

Let me check the Fanny Pack, Mrs. Mom said.

Mmmm... I think we left them in the room.

NOOOOOOOOOOOOOOOOOOOOOOOOOO!!!!!

Worse than my headache, Mrs. Mom's Magical Fanny Pack had failed. FAILED! That's never happened before. She's been toting her Fanny Pack around for about 20 years and it's never failed before. How could this happen?

I had to "suffer" through my headache, but I got my steak. It was good. So good I think I came back 6 times or so over the next few days. So what's the lesson here? Don't rush Mrs. Mom when she's packing the Magical Fanny Pack.

Really Dad? That's the lesson? That's not very helpful.

OK, try this. While you can't prepare for all the Stuff that Happens at Walt Disney World there are some things you can prepare for.

That sounds better.

I'm glad you approve.

So let's talk about some things you can do before you go on your trip of a lifetime to "be prepared."

The Park Bags

Let's start with what to pack for in your Park Bags.

I could make about a hundred different lists for what you need to take to the parks. But that would make this book way too many pages. So go over to the website where I've got a whole bunch of suggestions and lists from some of my friends about what they take to the parks.

What's in a park bag will change depending on the age of kids, the time of day, the weather, etc. Now that it's just me and Mrs. Mom, we'll only take the Magical Fanny Pack and leave the backpack in the room (especially if it's not going to rain).

What's in your park bag? Come over and tell us what's in your park bag!

The meeting place

One thing that's very important to PLAN for is what to do if you get separated. Where are you going to meet?

We only had one "episode" over the course of our trips when we misplaced someone. We didn't have a designated meeting place and it caused a little bit of angst. (That's a nice way to say, it caused a big meltdown.)

We lost the Grandparents. It's kind of a long story, so I'll move it over to the website.

SimpleFunMagic.com/Lost-The-Grandparents

The moral of the story is, always have a meeting place. You never know when someone is going to get "misplaced." You should designate an emergency meeting place in each park.

Be very thoughtful and specific about meeting places. "Meet at Cinderella Castle" sounds good until you look around Cinderella Castle. Cinderella Castle is big. Are you talking about down by the stage? Over by the wishing well? Down where the smokers smoke? Maybe on the back side by the wishing well, or by the entrance to Cinderella's Royal Table, or...

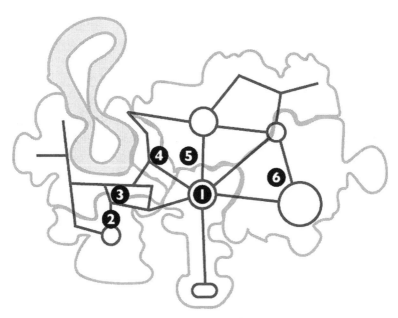

MAIN STREET USA	1 - THE PARNTER STATUE
ADVENTURELAND	2 - THE SPITTING CAMEL
FRONTIERLAND	3 - ENTRANCE TO COUNTRY BEAR JAMBOREE
LIBERTY SQUARE	4 - THE LIBERTY BELL
FANTASYLAND	5 - THE CINDERELLA FOUNTAIN
TOMORROWLAND	6 - THE FLOATING SPHERICAL ROCK

Get the picture?

A better place to meet would be, say, at the Partners Statue. That's very specific. Easily findable. Or maybe the rocking chairs at Town Square.

There are a lot of places that are good meeting places. We have a whole list of them at...

SimpleFunMagic.com/Meeting-Places

When it comes to meeting places, be obsessive. Walt Disney World is a huge place and it's easy to get separated.

If you go to the bathroom, state exactly where you are going to meet. Someone separates to go on a ride, set a meeting place. Every time someone goes to do something away from the group, always remember to set a meeting place.

This is important. Trust me!

The meltdown

Meltdowns are going to happen.

Sometime during your trip, even at the Most Magical Place on Earth, even with the perfect PLAN - somewhere, sometime, someone is going to have a MELTDOWN.

It might be one of the kids. It might be one of the adults, but trust me, someone is going to need a timeout.

What are you going to do then?

Long days full of over-stimulation and exercise will inevitably lead to a time when, even the strongest of us will need a break. Inevitably, breakdowns and meltdowns will happen. At some point, there will need to be some quiet time.

The timeout

There comes a time when a timeout is appropriate. I'm not saying that this happens all the time at Walt Disney World, but sometimes, it does. There are times when behavior needs to be corrected.

It's a lot more difficult when you are somewhere like Walt Disney World. Where is the timeout spot? How are you going to discipline the kids (or the parents) when on vacation?

This is something to think about BEFORE you leave home.

When the kids were growing up, we had a "timeout spot." It was a corner of the house where there was no stimulation. When the kids misbehaved badly enough, they were sent to timeout.

There's no such option at Walt Disney World. There's not a quiet corner of the house handy when you're at the theme parks. Even in the hotel rooms, there are a lot of distractions.

Giving a timeout while you are Walt Disney World is a hard thing. I'm not going to pretend that I have an answer for you. This is a very personal thing.

What I will say is that the best way to handle breakdowns and meltdowns is to try and prevent them. PLAN some rest time into each day. Know where cool, dark, relaxing, and semi-quiet places are for a quick recharge. Be on the lookout for the symptoms of someone who needs a break, then take one.

When someone was starting to breakdown or meltdown, what we typically do is STOP and take a break. Most of the time, that break would include a nap.

Sometimes, you just need a nap. Which leads us to...

The joy of napping

Taking a nap is a big thing for younger kids. We all know that, but it's also a good thing for adults.

If you have children under the age of 100, you probably should plan a daily nap.

Excuse me, Dad. I think there was a typo there. You said under the age of 100. Didn't you mean under the age of 10?

No, I meant 100. This isn't one of those typos I use sometimes to get your attention. I really mean everyone under 100 should probably have a daily nap at Disney World.

On our last trip, just Mrs. Mom and me, there were several times where I put myself in timeout and took a nap.

It was typically around 2 o'clock in the afternoon, I would get really tired and grumpy and need a break. So I would take a nap.

And just how old are you? You get a little tired so you have to take a nappy? How cute.

Hey, it's a scientifically proven fact that taking a nap is very good for you. I take a nap just about every day.

Scientifically proven? Since when?

I'm serious. Napping is good for you. Look it up.

I think you may be on to something here. Maybe I need to start napping. If I keep reading this book much longer it's not going to be hard.

That was just mean. Probably true, but mean.

Go back to the hotel

Let's start out by talking about the best way to nap at WDW. The best way to nap at Walt Disney World is to PLAN three or four hours out of the parks each day, to go back to the hotel and take a nap.

Yes, three to four hours.

Trust me.

I think I said this about 100 times already, but the best way to miss the crowds at the theme parks is to get to the park at opening time. Crowds will build until mid-to-late afternoon.

So, the best crowd strategy is to get to the park early, and leave when the crowds get big in the afternoon, then come back in the evening and enjoy the evening activities.

That works.

> *But Dad, I don't want to take 3 to 4 hours out of the parks. That's crazy. I'll miss so much…*

Deep sigh. (Yes, I literally just did have a deep sigh.)

We could have a big discussion on what's wrong with your statement, but I'll be nice and move on.

So if you don't want to take two, three or four hours out of the park, the next best thing is…

Taking a Power Nap

Speaking of scientifically proven…

Have you ever heard of a Power Nap?

> *Power Nap. I like the sound of that.*

You would.

One of the best ways to shrug off the afternoon doldrums is to take a Power Nap.

> *OK, it sounds cool, but what's a Power Nap?*

A Power Nap is a short 10 to 15 period of sleep that refreshes your brain and washes away the sleepy feeling that typically comes in the afternoons.

> *OK, that makes sense, but how do I take a Power Nap at Walt Disney World?*

Taking a Power Nap at Walt Disney World is pretty easy. Disney has built nice Power Napping Stations all around the parks.

The Power Napping Stations are strategically located in nice, cool, dark buildings. There are specially built Power Napping Chairs in each of these Power Napping Stations.

After about 20-minutes, there is an alarm that turns the lights back on, a nice attendant wakes you up and asks you to continue your day. These Power Napping Stations even come with some built-in, soothing background noise.

They really are the perfect place for the perfect Power Nap.

Power Napping Stations? I've never heard of them. Where are they?

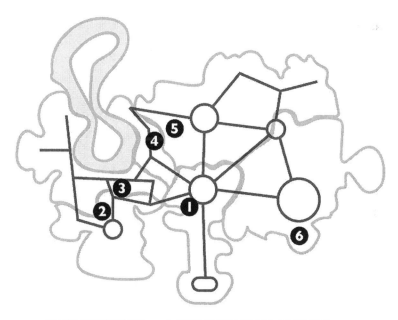

MAIN STREET USA	**1 - THE CASTLE HUB GARDENS**
ADVENTURELAND	**2 - THE ENCHANTED TIKI ROOM**
FRONTIERLAND	**3 - THE COUNTRY BEAR JAMBOREE**
LIBERTY SQUARE	**4 - THE HALL OF PRESIDENTS**
FANTASYLAND	**5 - MICKEY'S PHILHARMAGIC**
TOMORROWLAND	**6 - CAROUSEL OF PROGRESS**

Ooh, let me show you! Check out our cool Power Napping Station Maps!

SimpleFunMagic.com/Power-Napping-Stations

Those maps look a little different than the Disney maps. The Power Napping Station labels aren't quite the same.

Oh, they aren't labeled as Power Napping Stations on the Disney maps, but that's what they are. Disney wants to keep them secret so they give them code names.

The code names are cool sounding, like, the Carousel of Progress, Hall of Presidents, Enchanted Tiki Room, The American Adventure, Impressions de France, and Finding Nemo the Musical (the background music here is awesome).

Those are the best Power Napping stations. There are some secondary locations that aren't quite so good.

Good one Dad. Power Napping Stations. You got me there.

Dad's Bottom Line

Whew, that was a long chapter, but it's full of good stuff. Stuff you need to think about before you go. What to do in case of… Plan for it. Think about it before it happens.

Pack the essentials, and bring what you might need to the parks.
Know what you are going to do when a meltdown happens. Know where the Power Napping Stations are. Simple.

Thinking about stuff will make your trip Simple. It will help keep the Fun going. It really will enhance the Magic.

Trust me.

The Next Step

Wait! Wait. We're not done yet. We still have to put our whole plan together.

Uh oh… is this some sort of test?

That's right Pigment, it's time for the Final Exam.

THE FINAL EXAM
PUTTING IT ALL TOGETHER

"It's kind of Fun to do the impossible."
- Walt Disney

We've gathered all the information; we know Why you're going, we know Who's going, we know When you're going, we know Where you are going to stay and Where you're going to eat, we know What you are going to do when you get there, we know How you are going to get there and How you're going to get around once you arrive, shoot – we even know How you are going to get in shape for the long journey.

Whew. Deep exhale.

> *That sure was a long sentence Dad. Yes, we know all that stuff. So what's next?*

It's time to see how I did, I mean, how you did. Are you ready to create YOUR PLAN? Are you ready for the biggest test of your life?

The Final Exam

Everyone get out a #2 pencil. Now, take one of the Final Exams and pass them back to the student behind you. Don't open the test until I tell you to.

Having flashbacks are we Dad?

Ah, the good ole days. Final Exam day, one of my favorite days of the year.

OK, you're a little weird.

Yep. I liked test day. I'm pretty good at taking tests. Nah, I don't study much, I just have a mind like a steel trap.

I'm not sure I like that metaphor. But, as you're so fond of saying, that's not important right now. Let's get on with this.

Good idea, Pigment.

I guess the first thing we need to do is to actually pass out the test.

That's probably a good idea. But we're not actually in a classroom. How are you going to pass something out?

That's Simple Pigment. We've got it on the website. All you have to do is go over and download it.

SimpleFunMagic.com/Final-Exam

But Dad, but Dad. I hate tests! I know you like tests, but not me. You can't make me take a test. I'm a full growed up adult. I don't have to take tests any more. You can't make me, you can't make me.

So now, at the end of the book, when the rubber meets the road, when we're all done you are going to throw a fit. "Full growed up adult." You do know it's grown not growed.

Hey, you're the one writing this…

Good point.

Don't stress over the test thing. It's an open book test. Grab your "trip bible" or all of your notes or whatever you did to write things down. The "Final Exam" will just walk you through all of the notes, all of the steps, all of the information you've gathered and help you compile them into YOUR PLAN.

Trust me. The Final Exam is Simple. It's really Fun and the result will be... all together now... Magic!

Write it down

You just fill in the blanks. Yes, write it down. On paper. Print out the Final Exam so you can write everything down.

You should be able to answer most of the questions right from your Worksheets. There is no wrong answer. No one is going to grade your Final Exam (unless you want us to).

Get it all written down. This is important.

You got it? GREAT!!!! You have a PLAN!!! Aren't you proud? This is a big BIG deal. You have a good, well-thought-out, Simple, Fun, Magic PLAN for your Walt Disney World Vacation.

Share it with the world

Now, YOUR PLAN is all written down. You are ready to go to Disney World!

Aren't we forgetting one small detail?

And what would that be?

> *Something about sharing?*

You are so right Pigment. Thanks for the reminder.

Yes, now it's time to share your PLAN with the world. I want you to go up on the highest point in your neighborhood, climb the highest mountain, and shout it from the rooftops.

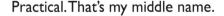

> *Mmmmmm, Dad! Really? Cliché-ville?*
> *I think you left out swim the deepest ocean.*
> *Can we get practical?*

Practical. That's my middle name.

> *I thought it was silly.*

Sticking my tongue out at you.

> *How adult. Can we move on?*

Look who's all growed up now! I'm so proud.

So, the first thing you need to do once you have YOUR PLAN all wrapped up is to share it with your travel party. Hopefully, they are right there with you helping you wrap YOUR PLAN up… remember, planning is NOT a Solo Sport.

If you would like suggestions on how to improve YOUR PLAN, or if you would like to help others make better plans, or if you want Dad to see what you've come up with. Head over and Share YOUR PLAN with all of us on our Final Exam Share page.

SimpleFunMagic.com/Share-The-Final-Exam

Now that wasn't hard was it?

Extra credit

OK, the serious time is over it's time to play.

At the very beginning of this book, back in Chapter 1, I asked you to tune everyone else out. To not look at other websites or books. I said that Dad's voice was the only one you needed to hear while you were planning your trip.

Since we're all done with the planning, now is a good time to, metaphorically speaking, unleash the hounds and have some Fun.

> *Do we really have to unleash the hounds? Those guys are annoying. They are yappy and they bite. Can't you come up with a different metaphor?*

Only you would complain about unleashing the hounds, Pigment. Metaphors aside, I promised to share some of my favorite Walt Disney World websites, books and tools and now is the time to let you "play the field." Is that better Pigment?

> *I'm good with that.*

So without further ado, here are a few, or a lot, of Dad's Walt Disney World favorite websites, books and tools.

SimpleFunMagic.com/Dads-WDW-Favorites

Dad's Bottom Line

I think we're ready to tie this thing up in a bow, to put it to bed. You've got this. You've done the research. YOUR PLAN is all neatly written down. YOUR PLAN has been shared. Congratulations.

The Next Step

Now it's time to talk about packing for the trip. We are about to experience the Scariest. Day. Ever.

> *I don't like scary stuff.*

Me either, Pigment. Me either.

20

SCARIEST. DAY. EVER.
PACKING DAY

"It's not so very scary. It's really not so scary.
Boo to you! Boo boo boo!"
- Mickey's Boo-To-You Halloween Parade*

One of the best commercials ever…

SimpleFunMagic.com/Too-Excited-To-Sleep

The day has come. It's time to go. Are you ready? Are you excited? Are you too excited to sleep?

SCARIEST. DAY. EVER.

The day before a Disney trip is the most exciting, busiest, and scariest day of the whole trip.

Exciting, I get. Busy, I get. But scary? What's up with that?

Yes, the day before you leave is the scariest day of the whole trip. Or maybe

Mickey's Boo-To-You Halloween Parade is a seasonal parade that happens during the Mickey's Not So Scary Halloween Party hard ticket event at Magic Kingdom on select nights each fall.

I should emphasize that a little - it's the **SCARIEST. DAY. EVER.**

You think I'm kidding?

Even Yoda* knows. Watch this. Luke is talking about going to WDW…

Come on Dad. That's not about Walt Disney World.

Yes, you're right, but it could be. Check this out. Remember that scene in the movie *National Lampoon's Vacation* where the Griswolds finally arrive at Disney World, I mean Wally World?

The whole family is so excited. Their dream is about to come true. They are at Wally World. They run excitedly across the parking lot (which I swear is a Disney parking lot). They run right up to the front gate only to find out Wally World is closed for maintenance.

How disappointing.

Clark punches Mickey, I mean Wally right in the nose.

(I would share the link, but there is some un-Disney-like language.)

That's pretty much what I'm talking about.

That scene haunts me the night before we go to Walt Disney World. Every time. I just know I'm going to have to punch Mickey right in the nose because Disney World is going to be closed and I didn't know it.

For me, the day before we leave for Walt Disney World the…

SCARIEST. DAY. EVER.

Uh, Dad… Has Walt Disney World EVER closed for maintenance?

*Yoda is a character from the Star Wars franchise. He's a Jedi master and mentor to Luke Skywalker.

I've said the day before you leave for Walt Disney World is the **SCARIEST. DAY. EVER.** Like 5 times in 372 words and you get stuck on WDW not ever closing? Excuse me. I think you missed the point.

No, Walt Disney World does not close for maintenance. It rarely closes for anything. Over the last 45+ years, it's only unexpectedly closed 4 times and never for more than 36 hours.

But that's not important right now…

Let's get back on track.

What we're talking about is the **SCARIEST. DAY. EVER.**

There are about a thousand things that could go wrong during your trip. The **SCARIEST. DAY. EVER.** is the day those things are going to haunt you all day long.

Remember that scary list from the Stuff Happens chapter?

The first five minutes after you wake up the morning of the **SCARIEST. DAY. EVER.**, these things will start running through your head, and will keep running over and over - all day and all night.

Trust me! Been there, done that.

OK, you've done it now, Dad. I'm not going. You just talked me out of it.

Wait, wait, wait… It's going to be OK. We're not done yet. Dad's here to help.

I'm just trying to prepare you for what is going to happen. It happens to me every time we go, even though I'm really good at planning. It's natural, and nothing to worry about, but it's going to happen.

We are going to spend the rest of this chapter making sure that you have solutions for everything that might come up, and even share some checklists that will help. That way, when you finally lay down at night, you'll know that you are ready for everything.

You'll still worry. If you don't, you probably need a show on the CW.

The packing list

One of the biggest worries you will have on the **SCARIEST. DAY. EVER.** is what to pack.

I could say that it's easy. Just throw in a couple of shirts, a couple of pairs of shorts, and be on your way. What else would you need?

Yeah, I know - underwear, socks, shoes, medicines, toiletries, swimsuits and more.

But packing for WDW is complicated. It's easy to overpack. It's easy to underpack. Should you take this? Do you really need that? What about...

So far you haven't been very helpful Dad.

Patience. I'm getting there.

All of us are different when it comes to packing, so it's hard to make a packing list that works for everyone, but we've given it a good ole college try.

SimpleFunMagic.com/Packing-List

The big thing when it comes to packing is to be sure to leave room for the souvenirs that will come home. I know a bunch of people that pack an empty bag just for souvenirs.

Earlier, we talked about the Park Bags. You'll want to be sure that you have everything that you need for the Park Bags too. (You'll find that in the Park Bag Packing List.)

SimpleFunMagic.com/Park-Bags

Carry-ons

The next thing to "worry" about is your carry-on luggage. What are you going to take on the plane, if you are flying? You don't want to pack too much in the carry-ons because you have to lug them around the airport.

Carry-on bags should have the essentials that you can't live without and that you don't want to pack in your regular luggage. Typically I'll carry on my laptop, my iPad, my charger cords, earbuds, medicines, and a change of clothes or two. You never know when the airline is going to lose a bag.

Usually some gum, Tylenol, a snack, a bottle of water (purchased at the airport), spare change and my keys somehow end up in my carry-ons.

Coming home is a completely different story. There are usually some bags with cool Disney stuff tucked just about everywhere cool Disney stuff will fit.

I know, some of you are screaming that you carry everything on. You would never, ever, never (I think there's a song there) check a bag on an airplane.

It's almost like you are reading my mind, Dad.

I know, creepy isn't it?

Not checking bags at the airport is your choice. Me, I don't like lugging luggage (boy that just rolls off the tongue) onto an airplane. For a short trip, maybe, but for a Disney trip, not for me.

Wow. The bags are packed. You're ready to go. I can't resist…

SimpleFunMagic.com/Bags-Are-Packed

You got through the **SCARIEST. DAY. EVER.** It wasn't so bad.

IT'S TIME TO GO TO WALT DISNEY WORLD!!!!!!

Dad's Bottom Line

Yes, the day before you go to Walt Disney World can be a little scary. That's OK. It's only natural. It's just your brain trying to make sure that you don't forget anything.

Just relax. Have some Fun. Jack in Dad's Packing Playlist and get it done. It's really not all that hard. In fact it's pretty Simple and it is going to lead to a whole bunch of Magic.

Now all you have to do is try to get some sleep. I know. You're…

The Next Step

Now it gets Fun. Next, it's time to go to the Most Magical Place on Earth!

Can I come too?

Good question, Pigment. Good question.

YOU ARE GOING TO A BETTER PLACE
TIME TO GO!

**"I have been chosen! Farewell, my friends.
I go on to a better place."
- Little Green Alien, Toy Story***

Wake up! Wake up! Wake Up!

It's time to go to Walt Disney World!

Come on sleepy head.

It's time to go. Get excited!

You've been waiting months, years - all your life for this moment.

You've been chosen. You are going to a better place.

*The Little Green Aliens are toys who worship the Claw in their arcade machine from the 1995 Pixar film, Toy Story.

YOU'RE GOING TO WALT DISNEY WORLD!

Yes, Dad. I'm all excited. Whoo, Hoo. But I'm a little unsure of exactly what's going to happen when I get there. Can you help?

Of course...

SimpleFunMagic.com/I-Can-Help

Arriving At WDW

The first few hours in Orlando may be the hardest part of the whole trip.

Hard? What are you talking about? Isn't it exciting?
We're at Walt Disney World! What's hard about that?

I know, it sounds so Simple. We're at Walt Disney World, let's just hop right over to the parks. What's the big deal?

It's not quite that Simple. Let's talk about arriving at WDW.

This chapter assumes that you are staying at a Disney resort hotel. If you're staying offsite, check out this link:

SimpleFunMagic.com/Offsite-Arrival

Disney's Magical Express

You've landed at the Orlando International Airport. Now the Magic begins (sort of).

The first thing you have to do is get from the airport to Walt Disney World. Oops. No. The first thing you will want to do when you land is to put on your MagicBands.

That's the "official" sign that a Walt Disney World vacation is officially underway.

There are lots of ways to get to Walt Disney World. Let's assume that you've chosen the FREE way. That's Disney's Magical Express.

Magical Express is a great service. It takes you on a Luxury Motor Coach (bus) from the airport to your Disney Hotel. Cast Members will even take your luggage and deliver it to your hotel room so you don't have to deal with it at all. How cool is that?

> *That sounds really great. One quick question. Can we just walk on, or do we need tickets or something?*

That's two questions, but they are good questions so I'll answer them.

> *You're the best.*

Yes I am. (Chuckle)

No, you can't just walk on to Magical Express. You have to have a reservation. There won't be tickets. Your reservation will be on your MagicBands.

> *Oh, so that's why we put the MagicBands on when we get to the airport.*

Now you're starting to get the picture. MagicBands are also wicked cool.

Now where were we?

Oh, yeah, landing and getting to Magical Express.

Magical Express is located on the bottom floor of Terminal B. Be sure you are in Terminal B. If you go to the bottom floor of Terminal A you will find rental cars and not much else. You'll have to go all the way back up to the arrival floor and cross over to Terminal B.

What about our luggage?

Another good question. You're on a roll.

Thank you!

You're welcome.

The cool thing about Magical Express is they will also grab your luggage off the plane and take it right to your hotel. You don't have to touch it.

BUT, that only happens if you use the Magical, Magical Express luggage tags. They will send you special luggage tags that if you put them on your luggage it tells the Disney to grab the bags and take them to the hotels.

It's really cool, but you have to have the Magical luggage tags.

This is probably a good place for our more information link. For more information about Magical Express go to…

SimpleFunMagic.com/Magical-Express

Here we go. You are on the Luxury Motor Coach (the bus) and your luggage is being taken care of by Disney. All is good.

Next you arrive at the hotel and the Fun begins.

Arriving at your Disney hotel

Arriving at a Disney Hotel is a special experience. If you are driving, you will be greeted at the "guard shack" with a friendly, "Welcome Home." This is one of the reasons I love renting a car and driving myself around at WDW.

Because of the "Welcome Home" at the guard shack? You're weird Dad.

Thank you Pigment.

If you are on Magical Express, your Luxury Motor Coach will take you right to the front door of the hotel. If you are driving, you will find that Magical parking space, or use the handy dandy valet parking (at Deluxe Resorts).

At this point there are two options.

The front desk check-in

Option One is going to the Front Desk and checking in. Checking in to a Disney Hotel is for the most part just like checking in to any other hotel in the world. The only real difference is that the Cast Member will be very friendly and will welcome you Home.

You will be given a packet of information that includes a map of the resort, which will have your room number marked on it...

If...

What do you mean with the if... thing?

You will get your room number if your room is ready. Check-in time is officially 3 or 4 depending on the resort, but sometimes even at 4 rooms aren't ready.

What do I do then??????

I promise, we'll get to that in just a minute, but let me talk about Option Two.

Online check-in

Option Two for checking in to a Disney Hotel is truly amazing. It's Online Check-in. It makes things really Simple.

With Online Check-in, you fill out a form online, and you're checked in. See? Simple. When your room is ready, Disney will send a text to your phone with your room number. You go right to the room and totally bypass the front desk.

That being said, I'm not a big fan of Online Check-in for first-time guests. There is something Magical about going up to the front desk and hearing "Welcome Home" for the first time.

You also get a good introduction to the hotel and where everything is from the Cast Member. If you have never been to a Disney Hotel before, the check-in desk is something everyone should experience at least once.

Also, if you need to make any changes, you will want to go to the front desk, even if you've done Online Check-in.

Drop bags and run

OK Dad, so we've arrived at the hotel. We're all checked in. Now what?

That depends on several things: time of day, whether or not your room is ready, do you have your luggage, do you need a nap, are you ready to go to the parks, are you hungry? etc.

Let's start with the your-room-is-not-ready scenario since I promised I'd talk about that.

If your room is not ready (or even if it is), and it's early enough in the day, you can head right on to the parks. That's right, go right to the parks, or to Disney Springs.

But Dad, I have my bags, what am I supposed to do with them?

That's easy. Just head over to Bell Services and drop them off. They will keep them and you can pick them up later.

If Magical Express has your luggage, you're golden. It will be in your hotel room later. Just like Magic!

If your room is ready and it's too late to go to the parks, go to your room. If it's really late (like 10pm or after), you may have to call Bell Services to get your bag if Magical Express brings it from the airport. (Magical Express drops the bags off with Bell Services.)

Getting to the parks

It's time to go to a better place. It's about to get Magical.

You are all checked in and it's time to head to the parks or Disney Springs. How do you do that?

Let's talk a little about Disney Transportation.

Disney Transportation is amazing. It's really Simple. It can be Fun, and there is even some Magic. Disney moves over 50 million people per year all around Walt Disney World. And they do it pretty efficiently.

How you get to the parks depends on which hotel you are in. Typically, you will ride a bus, but there are also boats and the best ride in the world - the Monorail!

How long will it take for me to get there?

That depends on both your hotel and your mode of transportation. We've created an ebook on our Disney Transportation page that shows how long to expect from each hotel. Check it out.

SimpleFunMagic.com/Disney-Transportation

Let's say you are going to a park. Hop on the bus/boat/Monorail and in just a few minutes you'll be there, right in the middle of the Magic. Simple and Fun.

Guess what?

YOU ARE AT WALT DISNEY WORLD!!!!!!

Talk about a better place. Does it get any better than this?

Dad's Bottom Line

Ok, you've made it. You are prepared. You have everything ready. And now it's time to have a ball. Remember Walt Disney World is Simple. It's Fun. It's Magic, so relax. Have Fun.

Don't forget to take a ton of pictures (and share them with us so we can be jealous).

SimpleFunMagic.com/Share-The-Pictures

Enjoy the vacation. It will be a great time, because you are at a better place.

The Next Step

We're not done yet. We still have one more thing to talk about. That's how to deal with that feeling that comes when you go home.

I get sad when it's time to go home.

Me too, Pigment, Me too!

I'VE GOT ADVBS
IT'S OVER, WHAT NOW?

**"Attention Travelers! Please remain seated.
Your vehicle is rotating backwards for your return to Earth."
– Spaceship Earth***

SimpleFunMagic.com/Yes-Its-Over

The Fun has come and gone. The Magic is over. Now what? Yes, as Johnny said, "we knew it had to end some day."

But that doesn't make it any easier.

The trip is done and next comes ADVBS.

> *Dad, what is ADVBS? It sounds like a really scary disease.*

You are exactly right. ADVBS is a serious disease. It affects almost 100% of Walt Disney World Guests.

You will start noticing symptoms as soon as you leave Walt Disney World.

*Spaceship Earth is an attraction at Epcot that showcases the history of human communication.

The symptoms will continue to get worse, and eventually, full blown ADVBS sets in - usually about 21 days after the last day of a Walt Disney World vacation.

Symptoms? What are the Symptoms? How will I know if I have it?

Oh, you'll get it and you'll know you have it. Trust me.

The more times you go to Walt Disney World, the worse the ADVBS is.

Dad, I just Googled ADVBS and I can't find it anywhere. It's not on WebMD or the Mayo Clinic website or any other medical page I can find. There are a bunch of international sites that say something about ADVBS. It doesn't seem to be a real malady.

Oh, it's real all right. I've been documenting cases of ADVBS for years.

Ummmm, Dad, I'm going to ask one more time, what is ADVBS?

OK, I've tormented you enough. ADVBS is After Disney Vacation Blues Syndrome. Yes, it's a real thing. It happens to everyone. It typically strikes right after a Disney vacation ends, but it can strike just about any time.

The symptoms are: depression, angst, the feeling that something is missing - things just don't work correctly.

SimpleFunMagic.com/ADVBS

There's only one known cure for ADVBS. You've probably already figured out what it is.

You think?

If you haven't I'm not a very good writer.

You think?

That was just mean.

You think?

Lol. Well at least one of us is laughing.

You think?

I think I need to put an end to this line of discussion.

You think?

(Heavy sigh.) The way to get over After Disney
Vacation Blues Syndrome is to…

*Oh, let me guess. You are going to say that the way to get over ADVBS is
to start planning another trip to Walt Disney World.*

Wow. That's a great idea. I would have never thought of that one.

Yes, the way to get over the Blues, the empty feeling, the sadness that
comes from missing Walt Disney World is to start planning another trip.
It's really Simple.

Oh, and in case you're not ready to start planning another trip, we have
a few ideas to help with the ADVBS. They won't cure it, but they will help
with the symptoms.

SimpleFunMagic.com/ADVBS-Cure

Dad's Bottom Line

You are going to suffer from ADVBS. Everyone does. It's a fact of life. It's
natural. It's treatable. I would say that it will get better with time, but that's
not true. It doesn't get better with time.

Yes, there are some stopgap measures (some really good stopgap measures)
that will help, but only a trip back to Walt Disney World will cure it.

As the Jefferson's use to say, "There ain't nothing wrong with that."

Whenever you are ready to start on "the cure" Dad will be here to help.

The Next Step

We've come to the end. As the old song goes...
"now it's time... to say goodbye..."

But wait. I think there's one more thing
I need to talk about and that's the "One
Simple Fact" that you'll experience on
your WDW vacation.

> *Good, because I don't like saying goodbye*
> *Dad. It makes me sad.*

Me too, Pigment. Me too.

STOP AND SMELL THE ROSES

"We ask honorary bugs to remain seated so the bugs, maggots, beetles and cockroaches can exit safely."
– It's Tough to be a Bug*

There is one more BIG thing I forgot to mention. Take it away Mac!

 SimpleFunMagic.com/Stop-And-Smell-The-Roses

Thanks Mac. What a great message.

Cool song Dad, but what's that got to do with anything? I've got to get this PLAN thing done. So why would you add in a song about roses of all things?

Because, you need to hear it. Trust me!

It's really easy to get caught up in the hustle and bustle of Walt Disney World. Almost every website, almost every Disney guru, almost

*It's Tough to be a Bug is a 4D show on Discovery Island at Animal Kingdom which is inspired by the 1998 Pixar film, A Bug's Life.

everyone that talks about WDW says the same thing.

"Hurry, hurry, hurry… You're going to miss something if you don't hurry, hurry, hurry…"

To which Dad says, listen to Mac. In fact, go listen to it again…

SimpleFunMagic.com/Stop-And-Smell-The-Roses

Let me tell you a little story. It's another story from our boy preacher at church. He's a good preacher and sometimes I even listen to what he has to say.

This one Sunday morning he told a really cool story… why don't I just tell it and quit writing meaningless words.

I can't wait for that to happen.

Stop it!

OK, here goes. Oh, I'm not sure about this story. It might be a preacher story, or it might actually be true. You never know with preachers. (I grew up the son of a preacher man so I know how it works.) But it's a really good story.

I'll be the judge of that.

The boy preacher told about a friend that had 2 young boys. I think he said they were 7 and 4. Let's call them Joshua and Caleb. Joshua, the older was a typical first child. He was always rushing around going from project to project. Getting things done. He was always the first to turn in homework, the first in line, the first at everything.

His brother was a little less… "energetic." Yeah. That's a good word.

Caleb was a really good kid. A smart kid, but he worked at his own speed. Whenever it was time to go somewhere, Joshua would be in the car waiting and Caleb would still be getting dressed.

The dad would get very frustrated with Caleb. He really wasn't a bad kid and he didn't ever act up or anything he just moved slowly. All the time.

One day Caleb came up to dad and told him he was going to start a club. Dad's ears perked right up. What club would that be, Caleb? I'm calling it the "Slow Club." I'm going to start recruiting new members.

Oh, boy Caleb's dad thought. I've got to see how this goes.

A couple weeks later, dad asked Caleb how the recruiting was going. It's slow said Caleb. I don't have any takers yet, but I'm still trying.

A few more weeks passed and it was time for church camp. The whole family was going. Dad was really interested to see how Caleb handled church camp.

The first couple of days things went about as you would expect. Joshua was always rushing to and fro, and Caleb was always the last one to show up.

On Wednesday of camp, dad asked Caleb again how his recruitment efforts for the Slow Club were going. Still no takers Caleb said, but how about I give you a one-day pass into the club?

What a great idea, dad said. That sounds like Fun.

So the next day dad followed Caleb around all day. When the lunch bell rang, everyone started running to lunch. Of course Caleb was his normal slow self with dad tagging right along.

As they were headed to the mess hall, Caleb stopped. Dad was just about to say something when Caleb pointed down at the ground and proclaimed, "Look dad. Look at that huge butterfly."

Sure enough there was a hand-sized Monarch butterfly right on the ground in front of them. Dad and Caleb sat there and admired it for a couple of minutes until it flew away.

As they got near the mess hall again Caleb pointed to something. He said dad "look… over there, in the tree line. There are a couple of baby bunnies." Sure enough right in the edge of the tree line were a couple of baby bunny rabbits.

Caleb and dad slowly made their way over close enough to almost touch the bunnies. They watched them for a couple of minutes until the bunnies hopped away.

"That's why I like the Slow Club dad", Caleb said. "I get to see things other people don't."

That's what Stop and Smell the Roses is all about. Seeing things that other people don't.

It's kind of like one of my favorite "old" songs…

SimpleFunMagic.com/Feeling-Groovy

It's really easy at Walt Disney World to fall into the rush, rush, rush trap and not take time to join the Slow Club, to make the moment last, to Stop and Smell the Roses.

When you rush, rush, rush, you miss an awful lot. Like…

• **The Beautiful Gardens** – When you think about "Stop and Smell the Roses", Walt Disney World is the perfect place. There literally are roses everywhere, along with lots of other flowers.

Disney has some of the world's best horticulturists. Everywhere you turn, there are flowers, trees, green grass, sculptured shrubs and beautiful plants. There's so much that you almost overlook them.

Several of the countries in Epcot have some spectacular gardens. The United Kingdom Pavilion has both a hedge maze and a butterfly garden. How cool is that?

Then there are the topiaries. Everywhere you turn there are topiaries. You know - The plants that are shaped like Mickey,

Minnie, Mater, Donald, Bambi, Tigger, and just about every other Disney Character. I wish I had one of those in my flowerbed.

• **The FREE Shows** —All day long, in all the parks there are FREE shows. Shows like the JAMMitors, British Revolution, Matsuizra in Epcot, the Tam Tam Drummers in Animal Kingdom, the Pianist at Casey's Corner, Dapper Dan's in the Magic Kingdom, and others. Notice a theme here?

No, not all of the shows are musical. You can find things like the chair stacker in France, the glass blower at Crystal Arts, I could go on and on.

And that doesn't even count the attractions, the fireworks, the parades, the concerts, the stage shows and lots more. You could spend a whole day in the parks and never ride a single ride.

• **Cast Members** – There are a whole bunch of really great Cast Members*. It's Fun to go around Epcot and listen to accents. Talk to them and get the stories of where they are from. Watch them interact with the kids. Most of them are incredible people with Magic to share.

One night I happened to be watching the fireworks from behind Cinderella Castle. A few minutes into the show, a Cast Member who was a janitor stopped and started directing the fireworks. He knew exactly where the next volley was coming and "called" the fireworks into the sky. It was enchanting.

I would think twice about Stopping and Smelling a Cast Member. That's a little weird.

• **The Cleanliness** - Walt Disney World is one of the cleanest places in the whole world. It's one of the things that make Walt Disney World so special.

The sidewalks get power washed every night. (That's why they

*Disney calls all of their employees Cast Members.

are wet first thing in the morning) and there is a trashcan every 30 feet.

I heard this at a convention at Walt Disney World. A guy was going to, oddly enough, a convention at Walt Disney World. The first day, he was walking down Main Street and spotted a guy in a suit picking up some trash. He went over and saw his name tag, it said "Michael." He asked Michael what his job was, Michael said he was "a janitor."

The next day at the convention, there was a speaker. It was Michael. Michael Eisner**. The guy got to ask a question during the Q&A and he asked Michael about the janitor thing. Michael said we have 50,000 janitors at Walt Disney World.

That is to say that everyone who works at WDW is a janitor, and everyone's job is to keep things clean.

They do a great job of it.

• **Fun at the Hotels** – You might be surprised at all the activities that happen throughout the day at the hotels.

There are different activities at each of the hotels. The Contemporary Resort has afternoon games for the kids. The Animal Kingdom Lodge has a viewing area of the Savannahs, where animals roam all day.

The Dig Site at Coronado Springs will keep the kids busy for hours. At Fort Wilderness Campgrounds, you can walk through the Tri-Circle-D Ranch where there are lots and lots of horses. At the Pop Century, you can learn to Hula Hoop and even do "The Twist."

In the evenings, activities include Movies Under the Stars. What could be better than sitting outside on a perfect Florida evening watching a Disney movie with the kids?

Michael Eisner was the CEO of the Walt Disney Company from 1984 to 2005.

I've barely scratched the surface of the Little Things around the Hotels. Check with the Front Desk for the daily schedule.

It's really easy to find things to do if you need a time-out and Stop and Smell the Roses. Just about everywhere you turn there is a little thing, a flower to enjoy, another amazing distraction.

Don't get so caught up in having to see everything that you miss a bunny rabbit or something else you'll be talking about for years.

Dad's Bottom Line

There is no better place in the whole world to join the Slow Club, to make the moment last, to Stop and Smell the Roses both figuratively and literally, than at Walt Disney World. There is Magic everywhere you look.

The Next Step

Wow. Now we're almost done. There's only one more thing to say. It's Dad's One Simple Fact.

I'm getting a little sad with this almost done talk Dad.

Me too, Pigment. Me too.

AFTERWORD
ONE SIMPLE FACT

"Ladies and gentlemen, boys and girls, on behalf of everyone here at the Magic Kingdom, we thank you for joining us today for a Magic gathering of family, friends, Fun, and fantasy.
We hope your Magical journey with us has created wonderful memories that will last a lifetime.
Walt Disney said that the Magic Kingdom is a world of imagination, hopes, and dreams. In this timeless land of enchantment, Magic and make believe are reborn, and fairy tales come true.
The Magic Kingdom is a place for the young and the young at heart. A special place where when you wish upon a star, your dreams can come true. Until we see you again, have a safe trip home.
Thank you, and goodnight."
– The Kiss Goodnight at the Magic Kingdom*

All good things must come to an end. It's a sad fact. Now before you interrupt and say something pithy that I will regret, let me stop you, if for no other reason than to spare my feelings.

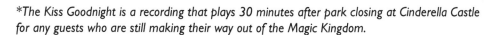

Reading my mind again are we?

Yep, and getting pretty good at it.

The Kiss Goodnight is a recording that plays 30 minutes after park closing at Cinderella Castle for any guests who are still making their way out of the Magic Kingdom.

Before we finish there are 3 things I want to say.

(Sigh.) How long is this going to take?

Not long, I promise, and I think you will like it.

OK, get on with it, will ya?

Thank you!

Here we go. First, thank you from the bottom of my heart for buying this book and reading it. I am truly grateful and humbled that you would take the time to read and consider what I've written.

Next, let's do a quick review, just to make my English teacher proud.

The review

A Walt Disney World Vacation starts with **One Big Truth.** Remember?

So, what comes next?

Remember YOU are going to Walt Disney World. This is YOUR trip. Not mine, not Uncle Jimmy's, not some know-it-all on a Forum. It's YOUR trip and YOUR PLAN!

Speaking of PLANS, you need a PLAN. A PLAN that is shared with the family and everyone going. A PLAN that is written down, a PLAN that has a budget behind it.

You get a PLAN by going Back to School and looking at Who, What, When, Where, Why and How.

Next, you get ready for the trip. You get in shape. You prepare for when Stuff Happens and finally you deal with the **SCARIEST. DAY. EVER.**

And then it's time to go. It's time to go to Walt Disney World. You will be Hot Stuff, the Conquering Hero, the King of the Lab, if you follow Dad's Simple Rules for Conquering the Theme Parks. (And if you Stop and Smell the Roses.)

Be ready, when you get home you will suffer from ADVBS.

There you go. That's the book in a nutshell.

> *Dad, you said three things. I'm almost afraid to say this but what's the third?*

Oh, yeah. I almost forgot the One Simple Fact.

One Simple Fact

The One Simple Fact is not to be confused with the One Big Truth. But it's just as important. Let me tell you a short story.

> *(Groan.) Another story? Can't you just tell us and move on?*
> *This is the last chapter.*

No! The more you interrupt the longer this goes on. Besides I think you'll like this story.

> I went over to visit my sister a while ago. There's nothing unusual about that, but on this visit she had just gotten back from Walt Disney World.
>
> My sister, her husband (my brother-in-law), their son (my nephew), and their 4-year old grandson (my nephew's son), I call him Joshua (because that's his name), had all gone for a week to WDW. They

were really excited to tell me all about it.

First, I saw my brother-in law. We talked for quite a while.

He was mostly griping about how much everything cost. He's kind of a Scrooge. He griped for a full hour about money and everything costing too much. Food, hotel, tickets. Then he complained about the person that planned their trip (not me). It didn't go well.

After a few minutes the son and Joshua came in and I got the whole rundown on the trip from a very talkative 4-year-old.

Then I went to dinner with my sister. She talked all during dinner about the trip. The good, the bad, the Fun and the not so Fun. It was one of the best dinners we've ever had together.

There were lots of stories about the trip, but there was one story that came up in all 4 conversations. Yes, even the one with Joshua.

The story that kept coming up was when Joshua went to the Jedi Training Academy. Joshua is a HUGE Star Wars fan. HUGE. He loves everything Star Wars.

One of the big "surprises" of the trip for Joshua was going to the Jedi Training Academy. It was THE thing they absolutely could not miss.

On their Disney's Hollywood Studios day, they got to the park early, and went directly to sign Joshua up for an early show. No problem, although my brother-in-law complained about how long it took, how hard it was, the walk, the Cast Member, why couldn't they do it online, and on and on.

In a few minutes Joshua was learning to be a Jedi. He was in heaven. It was amazing. Videos were posted on Facebook. Tweets came out on Twitter. Joshua had a blast. Even my complaining brother-in-law thought it was perfect.

Joshua made a Lightsaber (which he was really excited to tell me about and show me two weeks after the trip). He was still carrying it everywhere. He showed me exactly how it worked.

He was a true Jedi.

What does all this have to do with the One Simple Fact? Everything.

All three of the adults made almost exactly the same statement to me when they talked about the trip and about how exciting the Jedi experience was. They all said that the Jedi experience was worth every penny they spent on the trip.

That's it. That's the One Simple Fact. There will be something, some event, some ride, some meal, some experience that will make everything worth it.

There will be something that happens during your trip that you will say, "WOW that made the whole trip worthwhile."

My guess is that it will probably be something **Simple.** It will be something **Fun**. It will be something **Magic**.

Trust me!

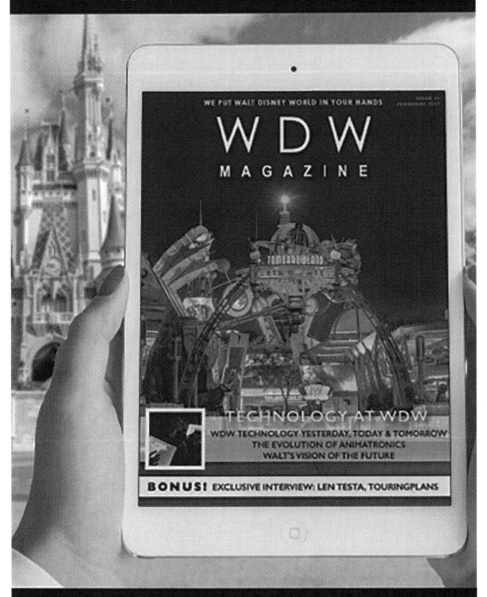

CHEAP DISNEY VACATIONS

ABOUT CARL (DAD) TRENT

Carl is a former Air Traffic Controller, who lives in Oklahoma with his wife, Mrs. Mom. Together they've taken trips to WDW as newlyweds, as parents with two kids (The Princess and The Man-Child) at every age from toddler to teen to all-grown-up, and even as empty nesters. They've even gone to WDW with an extended family of 15!

Carl knows Walt Disney World, and he loves nothing more than sharing his love of the Disney parks with anyone who will listen. Helping folks is something he was born and raised to do, and so creating Dad's Guide to WDW was a natural progression for this Disney nut!

In addition to Dads Guide to WDW, Carl is the proud owner and publisher of WDW Magazine (wdw-magazine.com), WDW Discount Club (wdwdiscountclub.com), and The Best of WDW (the-best-of-wdw.com).

ABOUT DADSGUIDETOWDW.COM

Since 2008, DadsGuideToWDW.com has been a leading online resource for stressed out families looking for help in planning their Perfect Vacation to Walt Disney World. On the site, Dad brings you Simple advice and Fun information to help you make Magical memories. You can count on Dad for honest, friendly guidance with Dad-itude to make your vacation - and the planning process - easy and exciting. Most importantly, Dad encourages readers to remember that it's all about YOUR Vacation, YOUR Memories, YOUR Way.